Flavio Bassi

The New Transport series - Supertrain project

Hotel-Train

Revolutionise night trains with a real rolling hotel

futurbooks

Copyright © 2022 Flavio Bassi

All Rights Reserved

ISBN: 978-88-31474-12-2

I edition, paper-book, softcover: September 2022

ISBN: 978-88-31474-13-9

I edition, e-book, epub: September 2022

I edition, e-book, pdf-7x10: September 2022

Futurbooks - Firenze

All photographs are from the indicated Author or Source

Cover image by: visualsofdana, Kari Shea, Flavio Bassi

The Reader-Writer Agreement

This work contains a series of innovative ideas, most of them invented by the Author, Flavio Bassi. If you read these ideas, find something that you hadn't thought of, and use it for work, business, research and/or commercial purposes, please feel *obliged* to contact the Author of this work and to agree with him on a fair remuneration based on the new ideas the Author gave you.

It is not about the law; it is about humanity. It is about the common sense of natural human justice, which comes before law.

In fact, it is not common, not easy, to invent a new object; however, if you use this new object, you could have big gains in some cases.

The Author gives you this book to read, but not to work with. If you work with it please remunerate the Author. If you do not, you go against the common sense of human justice.

And if you start your activity beginning with a natural injustice, what happens? Nothing is certain, but if the beginning is not beautiful, the next activity will be not as good as it could be.

So, if you simply contact the Author and talk about a small percentage of your net gains, you start with the right way. That percentage will be insignificant for your business, it will not slow you down at all. And if you will have no net gains, you will pay nothing.

STAGES FOR A NEW OBJECT	DESCRIPTION	IMPORTANCE %
FIRST IDEA	STARTING CONCEPT	S1%
FIRST SETTING	FIND BASIC RULES, PEOPLE, PLACES, MONEY ON THE BASIS OF THE FIRST IDEA	S2%
SECOND IDEAS	DEVELOPMENT OF THE FIRST IDEA ADDING SEVERAL NEW IDEAS	S3%
PROJECT OUTLINE	APPLICATION OF THE SECOND IDEAS WITH FIRST SETTING REQUIREMENTS	S4%
PROJECT OPERATIONAL	REAL PROJECT TO BUILD THE OBJECT ON THE BASIS OF THE OUTLINE PROJECT	S5%
CONSTRUCTION	OBJECT IS BUILT ON THE BASIS OF THE OPERATIONAL PROJECT	S6%
	TOTAL	100%

The Reader-Writer Agreement, importance of the different stages

STAGES FOR A NEW OBJECT	READER'S SHARE %	WRITER'S SHARE %	TOTAL
FIRST IDEA	S1R%	S1W%	100%
FIRST SETTING	100%	0%	100%
SECOND IDEAS	S3R%	S3W%	100%
PROJECT OUTLINE	100%	0%	100%
PROJECT OPERATIONAL	100%	0%	100%
CONSTRUCTION	100%	0%	100%

The Reader-Writer Agreement, shares of the Reader and the Writer in the different stages

Looking at the figures, first we need to assign an importance to each stage of the new object; then to define the share of the Reader and the Writer in each stage, based on one's own situation.

The Author, electrical engineer with applications in transport, management, tourism and natural architecture, is available also to further develop the outline project, or to think about other new ideas.

The contact data of the Author are in the "Contacts" section of this book.

If you disagree about this rule you should not read this work. Thank you!

Index

The Reader-Writer Agreement 5

Introduction 15

Should I take the train? 17

Legend 19

Part I - The concept 21

Chapter 1 23
Internal design

Idea 1.1 25
Double-deck, double-income
Level 1

Idea 1.2 26
Double-deck, double-corridor
Level 3

Idea 1.3 28
A touch of luxury
Level 2

Idea 1.4 29
A touch of luxury: Top-Of-The-Top-Luxe Suites
Level 2

Idea 1.5 32
A touch of luxury: Cheap-Luxe Suites
Level 3

Idea 1.6 34
A touch of luxury: panoramic points
Level 2

Idea 1.7 36
Real bedroom, real bathroom, real shower
Level 2

Index

Idea 1.8 38
Real restaurant, real lounge cafè
Level 2

Idea 1.9 40
Real cinema
Level 3

Idea 1.10 42
Real Personal Workspace
Level 3

Idea 1.11 45
Modularity
Level 3

Idea 1.12 46
Different passenger, different work
Level 3

Idea 1.13 50
Special luggages, special bicycles
Level 3

Idea 1.14 52
Special windows
Level 3

Idea 1.15 54
Special lights
Level 2

Idea 1.16 55
Special music
Level 3

Idea 1.17 57
Special materials
Level 3

Idea 1.18 60
Special perfumes
Level 3

Idea 1.19 61
Special accessibility
Level 2

Idea 1.20 63
One hotel, one entrance
Level 3

Idea 1.21 65
One hotel, many styles
Level 3

Idea 1.22 67
Natural architecture
Level 3

Chapter 2 69
On-board services

Idea 2.1 71
What about... shopping?
Level 3

Idea 2.2 72
What about... sport?
Level 3

Idea 2.3 74
What about... learning?
Level 3

Idea 2.4 76
What about... tourism?
Level 3

Idea 2.5 78
What about... art?
Level 3

Idea 2.6 79
What about... showrooms of innovative products?
Level 3

Chapter 3 81
Off-board services

Idea 3.1 83
Home-To-Home Luggage Service
Level 1

Idea 3.2 84
Home-To-HomeStation Luggage Service
Level 3

Idea 3.3 85
HomeStation-To-Home Luggage Service
Level 3

Index

Idea 3.4 86
Home-To-Station Luggage Service
Level 3

Idea 3.5 87
Station-To-Home Luggage Service
Level 3

Idea 3.6 88
Home-To-Station Transfer Service
Level 3

Idea 3.7 89
Station-To-Home Transfer Service
Level 3

Idea 3.8 90
Residential Station Lounge
Level 3

Idea 3.9 91
Residential Transfer Lounge
Level 3

Chapter 4 95
Economics

Idea 4.1 97
Different passenger, different strategy
Level 3

Idea 4.2 99
Different passenger, infinite fares
Level 3

Idea 4.3 100
Universal Transport Card
Level 3

Idea 4.4 102
Universal Transport Card on-board payments
Level 3

Chapter 5 105
Routes & Timetables

Idea 5.1 107
Undulatory Paths
Level 3

Index

Idea 5.2 108
Circular Paths
Level 3

Idea 5.3 110
Undulatory&Circular Paths
Level 3

Idea 5.4 111
Low Speed
Level 3

Idea 5.5 112
Day Use
Level 3

Idea 5.6 116
Forgotten Stations
Level 3

Idea 5.7 117
On Demand Stations
Level 3

Idea 5.8 119
On Demand Routes
Level 3

Idea 5.9 120
Stable Stations
Level 3

Idea 5.10 122
Personal Stable Stations
Level 3

Idea 5.11 123
Railway Cruises
Level 2

Part II - The train 127

Chapter 6 129
Layout design

Idea 6.1 131
Business Carriage
Level 3

Idea 6.2 135
Art Carriage
Level 3

Idea 6.3 138
Cinema Carriage
Level 3

Idea 6.4 140
Academy Carriage
Level 3

Idea 6.5 142
Sport Carriage
Level 3

Idea 6.6 144
Shopping Carriage
Level 3

Idea 6.7 145
Touring Carriage
Level 3

Idea 6.8 146
Family Carriage
Level 3

Idea 6.9 147
Bicycle Carriage
Level 3

Idea 6.10 150
Luxe Carriage
Level 3

Idea 6.11 153
Cargo Carriage
Level 3

Chapter 7 157
Experience

Idea 7.1 159
Available services
Level 3

Idea 7.2 160
Paid services and free services
Level 3

Index

Idea 7.3 162
Tickets and services
Level 3

Idea 7.4 164
The Gift
Level 3

Idea 7.5 166
Delayed passengers
Level 3

Idea 7.6 167
Room comparison
Level 3

Idea 7.7 168
Carriage comparison
Level 3

Idea 7.8 169
Complete rolling train
Level 3

Chapter 8 173
Business plan

Idea 8.1 175
Expected fares
Level 3

Idea 8.2 178
Comparison with the OBB case
Level 3

Idea 8.3 181
Replacement Carriages
Level 3

Conclusions 185

Destiny and Rationality 187

Contacts 189

Index

Introduction

In the last 40 years I have almost always travelled by train, ever since I was a child. After about the first 10 I began to observe trains more carefully, asking myself questions: "Why are they made this way? Why are they not made that other way?". In fact, this has become a characteristic of mine: when I see something interesting I think if there could be a way to improve it.

Questions overlapped with questions, year after year. School ended, university ended, I became an engineer, then a small business owner, I got married, a wonderful baby has arrived... but the answers were zero. Trains continued to be made as they were in the beginning. There were only minor improvements in important but secondary aspects; the basic substance of the trains always remained the same: carriages with seats. I had different ideas, though.

It was impossible to propose anything to the railway companies: they were mammoth giants, and when a giant goes its own way you cannot interrupt it, you cannot distract it, you cannot talk to it.

At the end I had so many ideas about innovative trains in my head that I couldn't resist. I had to do something.

And here I am. In this book I imagine to collaborate with a new railway company, focused on realising a new concept of night train: European, international, business, one-night-trips-oriented.

Given that trains will be business-oriented, they must contain bedrooms with bathroom and shower, restaurant, cafè, several meeting rooms sized for few seats, one (or more) larger conference room, company says.

The company's aim is to change the world of night trains, offering a new concept of real moving railway hotel; completely different from the old-style night train with sleeping cars.

Since that the company is new, its business plan provides trains composed by all-equal carriages (to compress costs in the first period).

What follows are my proposals in this regard, at a rough, starting project level. They condense everything I had in mind about the new night trains.

Should I take the train?

There are many reasons to say "yes, you should".

First of all, thinking about you: the comfort. Train, if well-designed, makes you travel without hassle. You can do what you want - read, write, work, have lunch, dine, rest, sleep, look at the panorama... and many other incredible new activities that we will see in this book. And you're still travelling.

The new Hotel-Train will be designed exactly to allow you to perform these activities and others in maximum comfort, at a level of comfort unimaginable in today's trains.

And as a second fact, thinking about others and the planet: the emissions. Any mode of transport has emissions, take CO_2 for example; but there are modes which have higher emissions, and modes which have lower emissions. The train is the *best* mode (apart from walking and cycling): we could say this on the basis of simple intuitive observations, but if we take some data from the "UK Department for Business, Energy & Industrial Strategies", for example, we see a 70% improvement over ferry-boats, and a 90 to 97% improvement over other modes. Other observers assign better values to boats, but the substance remains similar.

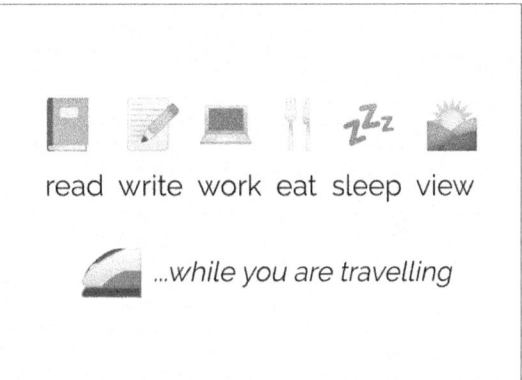

Example of activities which are doable on a running train.

CO2 EQUIVALENT EMISSIONS PER PASSENGER, PER KM	GRAMS	TRAIN IMPROVEMENT
TRAIN INTERNATIONAL	6	---
FERRY BOAT FOOT PASSENGER	19	- 68 %
ELECTRIC CAR MEDIUM SIZE	53	- 89 %
GASOLINE CAR SMALL SIZE (TWO PASSENGERS)	96	- 94 %
MOTORCYCLE MEDIUM SIZE	103	- 94 %
BUS	105	- 94 %
FLIGHT INTERNATIONAL	156	- 96 %
DIESEL CAR MEDIUM SIZE	171	- 96 %
GASOLINE CAR MEDIUM SIZE	192	- 97 %

Train emissions compared to other modes of transport

These two reasons seem unbeatable, for medium to long-distance travel.

Data from:
https://www.visualcapitalist.com/comparing-the-carbon-footprint-of-transportation-options/

Legend

Levels of innovation

Level 1: ideas which are already known in night trains
Level 2: ideas which are little-known in night trains
Level 3: ideas which are probably unknown in night trains

Notice: provided that the following chapters will contain a dense series of innovative ideas, almost all of them never seen in the railway world, it would be advisable to read slowly, without hurry. Otherwise the too dense novelties could disorient the Reader, and the real meaning and importance of each novelty could be hidden in the confusion of thoughts - producing at the end nothing more than a boring and useless reading. Instead, looking with attention at one innovative idea, rethinking slowly about it, trying to imagine what we could produce in the real tangible world with that idea... this is truly the experience this book would like to offer.

Part I - The concept

Here we see the starting ideas that will build, all together, the new Hotel-Train.

Chapter 1

Internal design

Part I - The concept Chapter 1 - Internal design

Idea 1.1
Double-deck, double-income

Level 1

Double-deck carriages provide more internal space than single-deck carriages; the extra space can be used to increase the number of available beds and to offer additional services. Even with an increase of costs due to the double deck layout, the total income should increase; this, if the customers demand will be enough high, higher than what is satisfiable with single-deck carriages. And this could be, if the new Hotel-Train will be successful in changing the night train world.

Double-decking has also the advantage of offering a more eventful and interesting train.

Note: not "double-income" but "increased-income".

OBB NightJet - Bernhard Beck

JR Sunrise Express - Maeda Akihiko

Examples:

OBB NightJet
https://www.seat61.com/trains-and-routes/nightjet.htm
https://www.dropbox.com/s/sjdblwbapwkgjkg/Nightjet-doppelstock.pdf?dl=0
https://www.360cities.net/image/city-night-line-deluxe-sleeper-schlafwagen-2007-germany

JR Sunrise Express
https://www.jrailpass.com/blog/night-trains-sunrise-express
https://www.youtube.com/watch?v=JgHplq6C64U
https://www.youtube.com/watch?v=oW3TPA5w2e8
https://www.youtube.com/watch?v=wcYQzzTT73Y

Idea 1.2
Double-deck, double-corridor

Level 3

In the said existing examples of night trains with double-deck carriages, Sunrise Express and NightJet, each carriage has a single corridor at a middle level; this corridor is at one side of the carriage, left or right, and from the corridor you can go in all the rooms. Each room has its own door on this corridor... but the upper rooms have stairs going up, and the lower rooms have stairs going down. So you have always stairs, to go inside your room.

Sunrise Express, staircase down to lower compartments - Solo Solo Travel

Not the maximum comfort; it could be an acceptable compromise if the stairs were very well designed. The design of the stairs is a crucial point, here, for a good result.

There is another possibility, the double corridor; it should be investigated. One corridor will be in the lower deck and the other one in the upper deck, similarly to what happens in the double-deck day trains.

But this way usually has stairs to go through the different carriages, which is not so good. So the quasi-impossible mission should be to design carriages with two corridors, upper and lower, but the lower should be without stairs. Inclined passages will be necessary.

There could be problems with the available height for the upper side corridor: the carriage cross-section should be "as much squared as possible", to have the maximum height on the left and right sides. Also, if necessary, the quota of the side corridor of the upper deck could be lowered a little using a sort of indentation on the floor just for it, to gain height. Alternatively, in the top-deck we could have a central corridor, instead of a side corridor; with a central corridor the rooms will be narrower, but perhaps they could be acceptable with a good design. This option needs to be better investigated.

If this double-corridor mission will be successful, the result will be: more space in carriages, maintaining a good comfort regarding the stairs. More people can stay in the Hotel-Train, with good comfort for everyone. At the end, more passengers should use the train.

Examples:

Rock train, good example because it has comfortable stairs
https://it.wikipedia.org/wiki/Hitachi_Rock

Vivalto train, bad example because of its steep stairs
https://it.wikipedia.org/wiki/Vivalto

Rock train, staircase - BJ Liguria

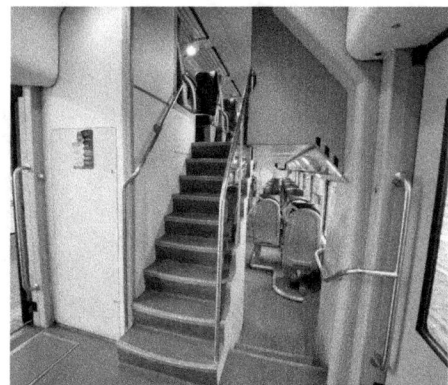

Vivalto train, staircase - Saggittarius A

Idea 1.3
A touch of luxury

Level 2

YellowSquare Firenze, roof swimming pool - YellowSquare

The new Hotel-Train could be business-class-only; or it could be business-plus-economic-class; or also economic-class-only; but in any case some, astonishing, luxury touches somewhere in the train should probably be necessary, if the aim is changing the world.

In fact, even new youth hostels have a wonderful, panoramic swimming pool on the roof, and are well refined (look at the "YellowSquare" in Florence, for example); and the same happens, more obviously, in business hotels.

These luxury touches, where could they be?

- in the general architecture; I mean, real bedrooms, bathrooms, showers, restaurants, etc., large passages, no stairs, interesting inner point of views during on-board walks... and so on; unluckily, all these things eat space;

- in the design of single visual elements, materials, lights, music, perfumes, etc; luckily all these do not eat space;

- in the presence of some de-luxe suites; which always eat space;

- in the presence of some panoramic points; which eat space or not, depending on cases;

- in the offer of new, never seen on trains, on-board and off-board services; which eat space or not, depending on cases.

All these points are discussed in separate ideas.

Examples:

YellowSquare
https://yellowsquare.it/florence/eat-party/?lang=en

Part I - The concept   Chapter 1 - Internal design

Idea 1.4
A touch of luxury: Top-Of-The-Top-Luxe Suites

Level 2

In trains, real de-luxe suites should occupy the whole width and the whole height of their carriage. This layout has no corridor; so it needs to be located in the very last position of the train, facing the rear, as it happens in the "Seven Stars" with an incredible painting-like large window.

Seven Stars - JR Kyushu

There is the possibility of de-luxe suites occupying the whole height but not the whole width; they take only one side of the carriage, leaving space for a shared corridor to walk along the train. Look for example at the "Shiki-shima"... it is like a complete flat on two floors... better this, or better the previous?

Shiki-shima - JR East

And there is also the possibility of de-luxe suites, with the whole-width and almost the whole-height (not the whole height but almost), inside middle-positioned carriages. This is possible because there is the necessary shared corridor, to walk along the train... hidden under some furniture! Look in fact at the

"Mizukaze"... its "The Suite" has this layout; it occupies a whole carriage (remember, there is always the shared corridor hidden under some furniture, under the sofa for example, practically invisible), it has also its entrance room with a private balcony on the side!

These are probably examples of the-top-of-the-top, like a complete residential apartment. They could be replicated in our Hotel-Train, if deemed right. Their price should probably be similar to the Etihad "The Residence" class, which however recently stopped because of the cancellation of all their A380 planes.

Mizukaze - JR West

Those Japanese examples are used as real railway cruises, also several days long. Maybe there will be a similar European market, for single night trips; or that market could be created from scratch (investigation necessary).

Thinking about the world tourism across Europe, could it be possible to have a demand of a luxury like this? There are two Orient-Expresses, the "Venice-Simplon" and the next "La Dolce Vita", which suggest that yes, there is a demand of top-luxury tourist train journeys.

Venice-Simplon Orient-Express - The Luxury Train Club

But here a question appears: will it be possible to mix top-luxury tourist and business travels? And maybe economy travels too? And in one-night trips? And if yes, will it be right? I'd say yes, but anyway an investigation on this subject seems necessary.

Part I - The concept   Chapter 1 - Internal design

Examples:

JR Seven Stars
https://www.cruisetrain-sevenstars.jp/english/
https://www.jrailpass.com/blog/seven-stars-kyushu-luxury-train

JR shiki-Shima
https://www.jreast.co.jp/shiki-shima/en/
https://www.japanstation.com/jr-east-to-debut-luxury-cruise-train-shiki-shima-in-may-2017/
https://www.railway-technology.com/analysis/featureonboard-the-shiki-shima-japans-newest-luxury-sleeper-train-5760864/

La Dolce Vita Orient-Express - The Luxury Train Club

JR Mizukaze
https://www.twilightexpress-mizukaze.jp/en/
https://www.jrailpass.com/blog/luxury-trains-japan#Twilight_Express_Mizukaze

Etihad The Residence
https://samchui.com/2021/03/14/the-end-of-etihads-a380-the-residence-and-first-class-apartments/

Venice-Simplon Orient-Express
https://www.belmond.com/trains/europe/venice-simplon-orient-express/

La Dolce Vita Orient-Express
https://www.orient-express.com/la-dolce-vita/

Idea 1.5
A touch of luxury: Cheap-Luxe Suites

Level 3

There is the possibility of a new way, a little less sontuous: using the top deck of the previously said idea of "Double-deck, double-corridor" carriages, at one end of the top deck we can put a whole-width suite by deleting one of the two carriage staircases, left or right; no problem with only one, it's useless to have two staircases in a night train because it is not like a crowded commuter train. This "Cheap-Luxe Suite" has not the whole height; but it has the whole width. We also could put two Cheap-Luxe Suites at both the right and left ends, if the carriage staircase will be set in the middle area, but this should be better investigated. There is to note that spaces for Cheap-Luxe Suites are available in all the carriages, not only in the carriage at the end of the train; and do not take much more surface area, compared to the ordinary cabins.

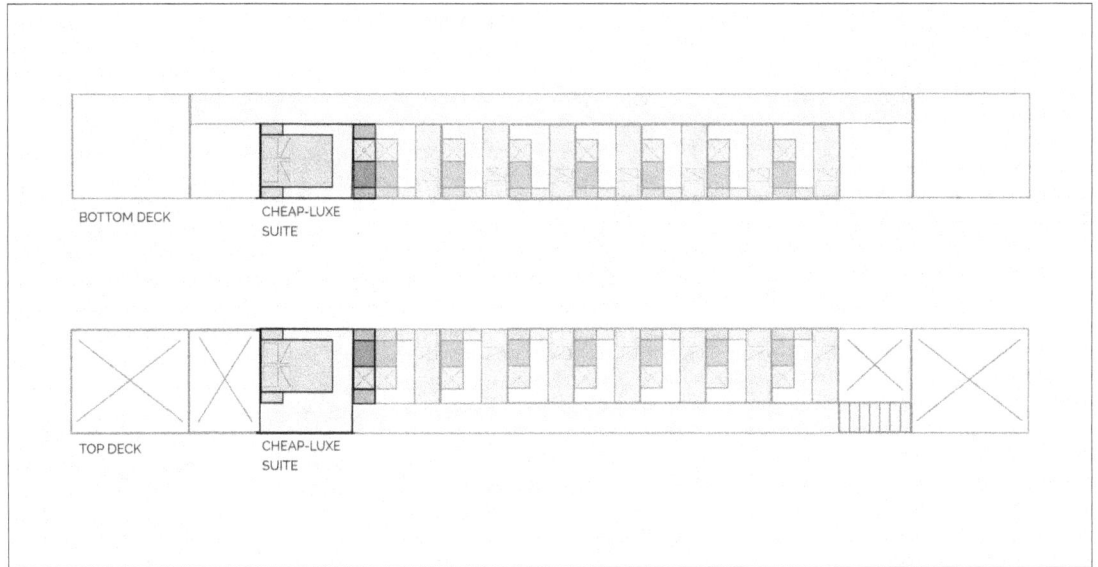

Hotel-Train, different types of Cheap-Luxe Suites in the "Double-deck, double-corridor" carriage layout

In addition, in both upper and lower decks, the space of two or more standard rooms can be used to place another type of Cheap-Luxe Suite, a little narrower than the previous one; this will have neither the whole-width, nor the whole-height, but it will be anyway larger than usual standard rooms. There is to say that similar suites, of the latter type, are already existing in several luxury trains of today, but not - as far as I know - in double-deck carriages.

So, these spaces could house a sort of de-luxe suites... for normal humans.

Providing such a large space to normal humans, passengers of the Cheap-Luxe Suites will experience a home atmosphere at a reasonable price; they should be pleasantly surprised; and this should create a series of positive actions-reactions, resulting at the end in the expansion of the number of people interested in the Hotel-Train (adding the ones which never withstanded the uncomfortable spaces of ordinary trains and want a little more than an ordinary cabin, to travel by train).

Idea 1.6
A touch of luxury: panoramic points

Level 2

Special (shared) panoramic points can be located:

- in large side windows for example in restaurants, lounge bars or anywhere;
- in a space which stands above the roof, or which has large windows on the roof;
- at the rear end of the train, in case of standard trains with carriages and locomotive;
- at both the ends of the train, front and rear, in case of "blocked-composition" trains with no locomotive and upper pilot cabin in the front/rear carriages.

Shiki-shima, View Terrrace - JR East

In my personal opinion (maybe wrong) it could be important to offer some special points of view; large side windows somewhere are surely necessary but probably not enough to change the train world, some of the other ones (roof/front/rear) would be required.

Mizukaze, Observation Car - JR West

About the said blocked-composition trains, they have advantages and disadvantages, and they can be constructed with distributed or concentrated traction; there is to say that the distributed system seems not recommended for the Hotel-Train, because it would have complex electrical and mechanical machinery close to passengers with consequent noise, electromagnetic and safety problems.

Examples:

Shiki-shima, at both the ends of the train, with large end/side/roof windows
https://www.jreast.co.jp/shiki-shima/en/
https://www.japanstation.com/jr-east-to-debut-luxury-cruise-train-shiki-shima-in-may-2017/

Mizukaze, at both the ends of the train, with large end/side/roof windows, plus balcony (!!)
https://www.twilightexpress-mizukaze.jp/en/
https://www.jrailpass.com/blog/luxury-trains-japan#Twilight_Express_Mizukaze

Blocked composition trains
https://it.wikipedia.org/wiki/Composizione_bloccata

Distributed traction trains
https://it.wikipedia.org/wiki/Elettrotreno
https://en.wikipedia.org/wiki/Electric_multiple_unit

Idea 1.7
Real bedroom, real bathroom, real shower

Level 2

All these points are fundamental but obvious, they will not be treated here. The new Hotel-Train must offer <u>real</u> rooms like existing luxury trains; absolutely avoiding - at any cost - any similarity with the terrible hospital-like sleeping-cars which resist to run in our days.

Ah! One moment... there is a couple of things to say.

First, in my opinion (could be wrong, as always) refined atmosphere, design and services are more important than sizes. Small rooms, small bathrooms, small showers could be a good compromise; apart from the case of the suites, standard residential sizes are not necessary. Certainly, everything must be very well designed to be comfortable and "real", even if small.

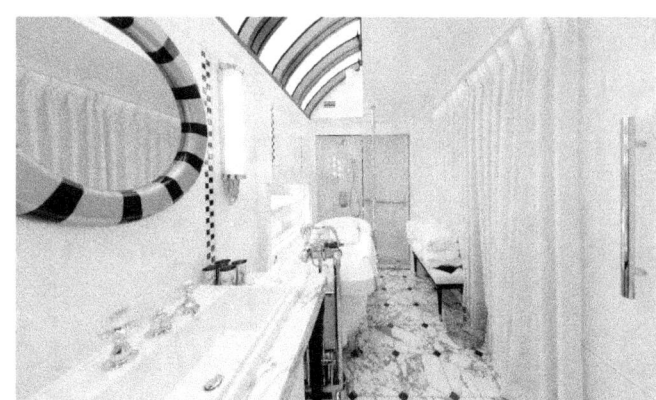
Shiki-shima, suite bathroom - JR East

Mizukaze, suite bathroom - JR West

And, about bathroom and shower: what is the importance of having them as private in all the rooms? High, very high. Everything possible should be done to provide them as private. Only if it turns out to be truly impossible due to the economical balance, it needs a serious investigation simulating spaces, costs and incomes in all the different possibilities (1 room with no private bathroom/shower? 2 rooms? 3... etc? And what about private bathroom only, with shared shower? And so on). Always remembering that the more private bathrooms/showers, the better for the passenger experience.

Examples:

Shiki-shima, look at the bathroom of the "Shiki-shima" suite...
https://www.jreast.co.jp/shiki-shima/en/

Mizukaze, look at the bathroom of the "The Suite" suite...
https://www.twilightexpress-mizukaze.jp/en/

Idea 1.8
Real restaurant, real lounge cafè

Level 2

These are very important, for me, if we want to create a true hotel atmosphere. A real restaurant to take dinner (or breakfast, or lunch), and a real cafè to relax, talk and enjoy. Even more than one (as it happens in the all-equal carriages layout) is good; or, better, very good: so that each restaurant and cafè could have its own style and characteristics, and so that every passenger could walk across the whole train to look for its favourite one... wonderful! It would be really like walking inside a real hotel.

Venice-Simplon Orient-Express, Dining - The Luxury Train Club

The cabin-only food (like the Italo seat-only food, for example) is a sad thing. It is necessary, instead, to walk outside, see other passengers, experiment different spaces, views, atmospheres... otherwise the trip is boring. You can't stay always in your space, during long journeys.

Obviously the quality of food is fundamental; the best on-board restaurant and cafè should compete with the most famous off-board ones, should be cited in the foodies'

Mizukaze, Diner Pleiades - JR West

guidebooks, if we want to change the train world. The subject is obvious and not treated here.

Shiki-shima, Dining - JR East

Examples:

Italo, wonderful train but with a sad and boring seat-only catering service
https://www.italotreno.it/en/the-train/italo-selection

Venice-Simplon Orient-Express, this is a restaurant! This is a lounge!
https://www.belmond.com/trains/europe/venice-simplon-orient-express/

Shiki-shima, this is a restaurant! This is a lounge!
https://www.jreast.co.jp/shiki-shima/en/

Mizukaze, this is a restaurant! This is a lounge!
https://www.twilightexpress-mizukaze.jp/en/

Seven Stars, this is a restaurant! This is a lounge!
https://www.cruisetrain-sevenstars.jp/english/

Seven Stars, Blue Moon - JR Kyushu

Idea 1.9
Real cinema

Level 3

This is a completely new concept. Very important, in my opinion.

A cinema, a little cinema for 10/20 spectators, does not take too much space. It needs only a small room, a good projector, a good sound system. Attention here: it cannot be a room plenty of screens, like the awful Italo Smart Cinema carriage (which in fact recently disappeared). It needs a <u>real</u> cinema, with cinema-style seats and one, only one, big, cinema-style screen. And not using ridicolous headphones! The sound has to be the cinema-style sound, diffused in all the room. And not sized for a lot of passengers! Only a little part of them will be interested in movies; also, the screen can't be too large, and in many passengers' long rooms it could become like a postage stamp.

Italo, Smart Cinema - dietrolanotizia.it

It needs a real mini cinema, nothing more, nothing less.

This would open some new world.

Let's imagine, a film festival of some subject, always different in the different periods of the year; and maybe with the subject depending on the destination of the train. The cinephile passengers would be in paradise. They will practice their cultural passion, watching real quality movies, discussing about them after the projection, in a little real cinema... while travelling across different lands. Space and time would be transformed to a different entity.

SNCF, Voiture-cinéma - Florian Pépellin

There is to note that a standard blockbuster cinema will almost surely fail; it will remain empty, because today blockbuster spectators watch their favourite movies in their smartphones.

But cultural movies, documentaries, art works, film festivals, discussions, awards... all this will probably find a new interesting home in the little Hotel-Train cinema room. Certainly, a proper off-board and on-board communication will be necessary to inform about this novelty.

This little cinema would be, for the cinephiles, like a workspace for the business travellers.

So this would expand the audience of night trains to another group of people: the cinema enthusiasts. Train-always for them, if railway cine festivals will be offered in a so cute, tiny, real cinema.

Examples:

Italo, wonderful train but with a useless Smart Cinema carriage (disappeared)
https://www.dietrolanotizia.eu/2012/11/su-italo-si-guardano-i-film/

SNCF Voiture Cinéma, a real cinema (disappeared... maybe it was so big that the screen was too small from a distance?)
https://www.lesuricate.org/etait-voiture-cinema-de-sncf/
https://old.reddit.com/r/trains/comments/ilfwhw/interior_of_sncfs_cinema_car/
https://www.patrimoine-ferroviaire.fr/sncf-voiture-cinema-sux-51-87-89-80-066-2/

Part I - The concept   Chapter 1 - Internal design

Idea 1.10
Real Personal Workspace

Level 3

Here we are launching towards the stars... let's explain from the beginning; it's not so simple.

In the usual concept of train workspaces (meeting rooms for around 5-6 places, conference rooms for 10-20 or more; which have been already experienced by standard railway companies, I don't know with what results) I see something... crooked.

In fact: there is surely a high demand of business passengers; but how many of them will travel in group, to work *together* during the trip?

And also: how much of them work *together* during the ordinary days? They usually work in their offices, with some space dedicated only for them; and only sometimes they have some discussion to share with colleagues.

The occasions of group working, or big conferences, are not so much even in the off-board world; why they should practice those few occasions exactly in a moving train?

It's almost impossible to move several colleagues in the same train... and to go where? Why should they go to the same destination, all together? They are not schoolmates. Usually the businessmen travel to their business locations alone or in a group of two.

FS Press&Conference, conference room - Davide Galli

Frecciarossa 1000, meeting room - Florian Buechting

"But we could use the same meeting or conference room sharing them with different passengers, each of them working alone by itself!"

We could, but that does not seem a proper "work"... That seems distraction, confusion, waste of time.

Work is work: it needs concentration, personal space to think and do without distractions.

In other words, I personally don't believe in coworking-style open space offices. It is very nice to have social spaces close to the working place; but the single working place needs to be personal, in my opinion.

Frecciarossa 500, meeting room - TheFlyingDoctor

Sometimes meeting rooms and conference rooms can be useful; but only in special occasions, not in all the days. While trains travel all the days.

So, I would replace the meeting rooms and conference rooms with another concept: <u>real</u> "Personal Workspaces".

What I mean, with Personal Workspace? Not a table over a bed, where maybe the businessman should seat on the bed to use the pc on that table. This does not seem business level.

It needs, simply, a real table (even a small one could be a good compromise), without beds below, and a real chair.

Where that table/chair set can be located? Inside the bedroom could be a possibility; but it is sad to stay always in the same place, as said before. So it is better to provide small bedrooms that are only bedrooms, and separate small personal office rooms with table/chair to work. In fact, I just deleted meeting and conference rooms, so there should be space enough to put those small personal offices.

If we give these little but real on-board offices, businessmen will experience that they can travel and, at the same time, work; exactly as they were in their, larger, off-board offices. As far as I know, no train, today, provides a real, personal, separate office like this... while in our times the so-called smart working, or remote working, is rapidly increasing. So, again, the pleasant surprise, the positive actions/reactions, and the

Hotel-Train, Personal Workspace will look like this - Ryan Ancill

consequent possible expansion of passengers market. Train-always, if they can do their real work during business (or leisure) travel, multiplying the possibilities during the same time.

"Hey! This way where are meeting rooms and conference rooms? We said we wanted them, even if only for special occasions. Here they are disappeared!"

No, they are not disappeared. Thanks to the next idea, Modularity, they can reappear when needed...

Examples:

FS Press&Conference conference room, beautiful but basically never used and canceled like new
https://www.ferrovie.info/index.php/it/34-correva-l-anno/2651-giugno-1988-le-officine-di-cittadella-consegnano-la-carrozza-press-conference
https://scalaenne.wordpress.com/2011/04/16/gran-comfort-e-grand-confort/
http://www.tplitalia.it/articoli/img/22032014-01/017-800.jpg
https://yewtu.be/watch?v=H6GLxFr8uBw

Trenitalia Frecciarossa 1000 meeting room, beautiful but probably always empty as in these photos
https://www.seat61.com/trains-and-routes/paris-to-milan-by-train.htm
https://www.uponarriving.com/trenitalia-executive-class-frecciarossa-1000-review

Trenitalia Frecciarossa 500 meeting room, beautiful but probably always empty as in these photos
https://travelupdate.com/review-trenitalia-executive-class-frecciarossa-rome-florence/
https://www.frompointato.com/2014/04/06/trenitalia-frecciarossa-executive-class-review-microwave-pasta-on-the-italian-high-speed-express/

Idea 1.11
Modularity

Level 3

Here we are in orbit. Now: there is the known problem of the railway carriage certifications, which crystallises the carriage structure. If I have different carriages, I need different certifications; and if I change something, I need another certification. And so on. Too expensive, so it is better to have all-equal carriages, and without changing anything.

But let's imagine, could we certificate modular walls and items? I mean, ok, there is the fixed main structure with windows, stairs, bedrooms, bathrooms, restaurants, cafès; but could it be possible to have a certification with demountable/mountable secundary walls somewhere? And demountable/mountable tables and chairs too?

If yes, all the space of the said Personal Workspaces will be a totally flexible open space.

In fact, remember, any Personal Workspace require only a set of walls/table/chair. So it will be easy to take, on demand, some Personal Workspaces and transform them in a bigger space, such as an office for two colleagues, a meeting room, a bigger conference room... or even something else a bit different... which will be treated in some next ideas.

Hotel-Train, Personal Workspace enlarged with Modularity will look like this - LinkedIn Sales Solutions

Idea 1.12
Different passenger, different work

Level 3

Here, I know, we are heading to the far space.

Let's return for a moment at the said Personal Workspace point.

Everyone, when talking about the work aboard the trains, thinks the same picture: dark jacket, clear shirt; a tie, sometimes (dark); laptop computer. Formal style, silence, internet connection always on, etc. The businessman.

Hotel-Train, Personal Workspace for businessman will look like this - Andreas Dress

Are businessmen enough to make the whole train full, all year round?

I don't know exactly but at a first sight... I doubt.

So, it could be advisable to look for other categories of passengers too. And in fact, there are also other categories of workers around here.

What works could be developed aboard the trains, in some Personal Workspace (which can be small or large, thanks to the said Modularity idea)?

Let's build a rough, fast list of works, other than business, that are doable on the train:

- painting;
- writing;
- reading (is it a work or not... yes, sometimes it could be);
- sculpting (well... not sure, because of carriage vibrations... investigation required);

Hotel-Train, Personal Workspace for painter will look like this - Laura Adai

- playing musical instruments and/or singing (if the space is well sound-proofed);
- music composing and/or editing;
- photo/video shooting and/or editing;
- studying;
- researching ("hey! this is not valid, it's like the businessmen!" ...well, maybe yes...);
- remote working ("hey! this is not valid, it's like the businessmen!" ...well, maybe yes...);
- building infinite types of handicraft articles (...why not?);
- professional sportingmen training (...why not?);
- teaching (...why not?);
- learning (the other side of teaching);
- inventing / dreaming (...why not ?);
- baby-sitting (the endless and unremunerated work of mums and dads);
- ok, now I stop here... others maybe.

In brief, every work which is done using no more than "little" tools and objects, and which is not dangerous, can be developed inside the Personal Workspaces of our new Hotel-Train.

So, what does it mean?

It means that each line of the previous list is a new world of possible passengers, where the Hotel-Train's business could expand.

In fact, the workers of each line of the previous list will find the night train trip useful; because they can work here, as if they were at their own ordinary off-board workspace, while travelling. Gaining time and arriving at destination without noticing the travel.

Obviously this is useful only if there is enough working time during the trip; and this is the case of the longer journeys, when the trip has some day hours, in addition to the night time.

Hotel-Train, Personal Workspace for writer will look like this - Hannah Holinger

Hotel-Train, Personal Workspace for reader will look like this - Tim Wildsmith

Hotel-Train, Personal Workspace for musician and singer will look like this - Luwadlin Bosman

The journey could even be a pleasure journey, a vacation; if the workers can work travelling, they gain always a day of work: the vacation starts later, after the arrival at destination (and the same happens on return). And also, the work during the journey could be a new, interesting, tasty experience (if the carriages are well designed).

As already said in other ideas, the result is the same: train always for those workers, when they can find a train with a workspace which is suitable for them; the train journey will be more comfortable, enjoyable and convenient.

Hotel-Train, Personal Workspace for photographer and video maker will look like this - Szabo Viktor

Hotel-Train, Personal Workspace for student will look like this - Green Chameleon

Hotel-Train, Personal Workspace for music composer will look like this - Luis Gherasim

Hotel-Train, Personal Workspace for artisan will look like this - Annie Spratt

Part I - The concept	Chapter 1 - Internal design

Hotel-Train, Personal Workspace for sportingman will look like this - Jonathan Borba

Hotel-Train, Personal Workspace for dreamer will look like this - Brad Starkey

Hotel-Train, Personal Workspace for teacher and learner will look like this - Wonderlane

Hotel-Train, Personal Workspace for mum and dad will look like this - Picsea

Part I - The concept   Chapter 1 - Internal design

Idea 1.13
Special luggages, special bicycles

Level 3

Oh, finally back to Earth. This should be not treated here, because it's so simple and obvious. It is so simple and obvious that railway companies never offered it properly. The point is: it needs space for bigger-than-usual luggages. The train/carriage design must consider this fact. Not only ordinary big suitcases; sometime there is something special to move. In fact, what do we do with cars? We carry "special-luggages" so often. So, why not in trains too?

What you carry in your car, you must be able to carry in the new Hotel-Train - Nikolay Loubet

Remember the previously said Modularity idea, which should be perfect here. Some Personal Workspace could be converted in compartment for special luggage, when needed. Certainly, the carriage design must consider this fact since the beginning.

And often, very often, there is a bicycle. The European-scale night trains would be paradise, for the return at home of the international bicycle travellers... like me. Which are a lot, because City Night Line had always the bicycle space sold-out when I tried to book.

The international bicycle travellers are in fact another world where night train business could expand... using the Modularity idea (without the Modularity, there could often be waste of spaces). But attention here: bicycles must not be hung on a hook like a ham! If bicycles are hooked (as railway companies almost always demand) they are ruined, and in addition hooking them is difficult and dangerous when the bicycle is heavy. After years of

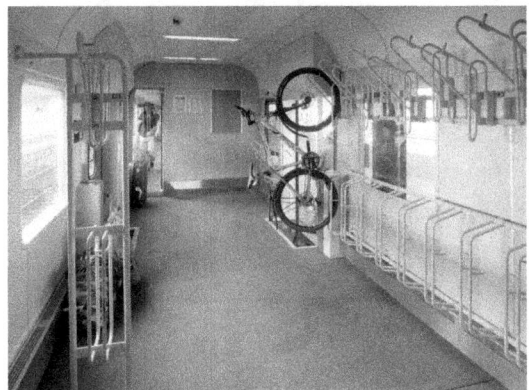
City Night Line, bicycle hooked like a ham on board the train - Falk2

frustration with bicycle transport on trains I can strongly affirm this: let's give bicycles the dignity of bicycles. They must have their own space on the floor, with both the two weels on the floor.

So, in our new Hotel-Train, the space of some Personal Workspaces will be set as parking for bicycles and/or storage for special luggages, depending on requests. When there are neither bicycles nor special luggages to carry, that space will be set differently and used for other purposes.

Idea 1.14
Special windows

Level 3

This is a completely new concept, probably never seen on trains. It is a fun-da-men-tal concept for the good result of our new Hotel-Train. The windows: what shape? What size? Where to put them?

If we look at the trains, it seems that the windows occupy as much space as possible all along the side walls, always. Compartments, restaurants, corridors... always. If you look at the side walls you see always the outdoor view. Ok, this is for the ordinary trains. But look at the previous "A touch of luxury: Top-Of-The-Top-Luxe Suites" paragraph, look at the photos of luxury trains: those photos come from their best top luxe accomodations. And they are all - none excluded - full of super large windows all along the side walls, like the ordinary trains. Why? Why are they like ordinary trains? I can't understand, why?

Window without dignity - DB Autozug GmbH

"...hey! Don't you know? Modern buildings have glass-only walls towards outside!"

Yes this is a fact. But modern buildings have glass-only walls, while here we have train-windows; that are different from glass-walls. Train-windows have their own shape and big structural external parts around them, they don't occupy the whole wall. And in addition, we are in a moving train, not in a fixed building; are we sure that passengers like to see moving landscape *always*, during their stay on board the train? I doubt... it seems to me that, during a long-distance journey, it would be better to have both opportunities to see large views of moving landscape, and

Window with dignity - Rob Wingate

opportunities to see interior decoration of rooms without those big, distracting, running views through the windows.

My point is that luxury trains are reminiscent of standard trains, having those kinds of big windows everywhere. Instead our new Hotel-Train must be an hotel, before it is a train. It should not recall ordinary trains.

Finally this is my proposal about windows: let's design small windows, with a traditional building style. No attempt to imitate glass-walls (apart from special panoramic points). No walls covered by large windows everywhere. Let's give walls the dignity of walls and windows the dignity of windows. A wall can be covered with a wonderful fragrant wood, can contain a library, a wardrobe, a painting, a flower... and then a medium-small window, beautifully refined, maybe inside a frame as it was a painting too.

If the light is not enough, because the window is too small, we can use some translucent openings to provide more light while remaining in a cosy environment. Roof openings can also be considered.

This would produce the real surprise in passengers: they live in a real room, like they were in a traditional building... but when they approach what looks like a luminous, transparent painting... *now* they see the world outside, moving around them. This experience should build the memory of the Hotel-Train.

Idea 1.15
Special lights

Level 2

Normal elements of design, here. It needs a lighting design, to create the right atmosphere. It is fundamental for a good result.

What I have important to say is only one thing. Never put that line of boring, all-equal lights along carriages, like it is in the ordinary trains. Each point, each area, needs its attention, its spot light, its mood.

Examples:

JR Seven Stars - this is a lighting design!
https://www.cruisetrain-sevenstars.jp/english/

Seven Stars, lighting atmosphere - JR Kyushu

Idea 1.16
Special music

Level 3

Normal elements of design, here too; but probably unknown in trains. It needs a music design, to create the right atmosphere. It is fun-da-men-tal for a good result.

Only few things to say here.

First, music played live by a musician would be advisable for the top lounge or the top restaurant of the Hotel-Train, at least at some time.

Second, never put the same music all along the train. It would be boring, disturbing... Each point, each area, needs its attention, its spot music, its mood.

And third, music has to be used with discretion. Only few spots needs music: some cafès/lounges; the bathrooms/showers (it would be complicated to treat here this curious fact, but based on my personal experience I firmly believe that this greatly increases the enjoyment of the whole trip); the private bedrooms and workspaces, on demand obviously; and maybe others to investigate better.

Seven Stars, Blue Moon piano - The Luxury Train Club

Arrival and departure music

There is an important exception: close to arrivals and departures it's nice, it's very nice, to have the same music all along the train. A music which is related to the place where the train is arriving/departing. This focuses the attention of passengers on these special moments: arrivals and departures are so special... they are instants in which the whole life changes. Those few minutes of nice, interesting, related-to-place music create a symphony, a memory, which then will mark the whole journey. It should result an increase in general interest, enjoyment, satisfaction.

Examples:

JR Seven Stars - its Blue Moon lounge offers live piano music
https://www.cruisetrain-sevenstars.jp/english/

Idea 1.17
Special materials

Level 3

Here's, this is another fun-da-men-tal point for a possible success.

It is well-known that high quality spaces use natural, warm, materials; this because warm natural materials not only look good, but have also a good perfume. Look at the scale of the ordinary offices, for example: basic worker = white plastic + black plastic; medium worker = fake leather + fake wood; top worker = real leather + real wood (so hilarious... but sadly true).

Golden Eagle, natural and warm surface materials - The Luxury Train Club

So, we want to change the train world, right? So, no plastic, no fake wood etc. Only real, pure, warm natural materials.

I say "warm" to exclude metal, which could be considered "natural", but it is to avoid. It is so cold, so poor, if used inside...

But this is well-known also in existing quality trains; or, better, in the luxury ones: all of them use real natural woods and warm surface materials almost everywhere, inside.

Provided that we want to offer a similar service, a railway hotel even if not so luxury, we must do the same. This is because of a simple but important fact: natural warm materials do not eat space. And we should do all we can to offer the maximum quality, with the not-eater-of-space things. Because our enemy is the space, our enemy is the fact that if we want to raise up the level, for example with substantial bathrooms and showers, we have to eat space. So when we find something that raise up the level without eating spaces, that thing is our alley and we must develop it at the maximum.

Oh, I'm sorry for the intonation... it seems a teacher, an expert... I am only a dreamer. Sorry again.

Now. There are some categories of materials in trains: structural, external surface, internal surface, insulators. Technical requirements usually decide most of the structural and external surface ones: steel, steel, and steel. Sometimes maybe a bit of aluminium (I don't know if carbon mixtures and company have arrived in trains yet, anyway I trust only on steel, aluminium and similar). So we can decide only about internal surface and... insulators.

This is the point. About internal surface, as said, all luxury trains use wood and similar natural warm materials. Ok, But what about insulators?

I suspect the answer: Polypropylene, Polyethylene, Polystyrene and so on. The usual plastic, synthetic materials used in all the vehicles and buildings. From cheap to luxury, practically everyone uses the same, horrible, things that everyone would reject if they were used for visible and touchable furniture. This should be, probably, because insulators are hidden, so the buyers - poor or rich - do not see them. Another hilarious-but-sadly-true point.

Polystyrene, would you use it as a bed? - Acdx

Here is my proposal, never seen in trains (or better, never seen in any kind of vehicle): could we use natural architecture materials in insulators, in addition to the natural materials used in internal surface materials? The result would be:

- more comfortable internal environment;
- better internal perfumes;
- "greener" vehicles;
- competitive advantage regarding to the competing trains, even luxury ones; which, I am almost sure, do not even know the possibility of having natural materials in insulators (certainly, a proper and not easy communication will be needed here, to communicate the value of natural insulators and gain this competitive advantage).

Cork, one of the best natural insulators - Sadenda

Examples:

Golden Eagle
https://www.goldeneagleluxurytrains.com/

Polystyrene
https://en.wikipedia.org/wiki/Polystyrene

Cork
https://en.wikipedia.org/wiki/Cork_(material)

Idea 1.18
Special perfumes

Level 3

This is another normal element of fine design, probably unknown in trains. Here it needs a perfume design, to create the right atmosphere. It is fun-da-men-tal for a good result.

The awful smell of the ordinary trains (apart from the newest ones, which have been greatly improved) must be absolutely avoided, otherwise it is impossible to reach any result; most of the people simply do not travel by train and go elsewhere, because of that smell (...I think).

Lavender, natural flower fragrance - Sharon McCutcheon

Using the previously said natural materials, treated with natural waxes and oils, the most should be done. If a perfume special design is added, everything should work perfectly.

What I have important to add here is a couple of things.

First, the dynamic. Each spot must have its fragrance. If the same one is placed all along the train, it will result a dramatically terrible experience. This fact should not be underestimated; perfumes communicate subtly, imperceptibly, and contribute to forming our sentiments.

And second, please never use hard and/or synthetic perfumes. They could be pleasant at first, but after few time they could become boring, and after another few time repellent. Use natural flowers, natural leaves, natural oils and natural fragrant materials like simple wood for example (cedar or others), to be stably attractive. Perfumes must be fresh, light and natural. And they must be only barely perceptible.

Examples:

Lavender
https://en.wikipedia.org/wiki/Lavandula

Idea 1.19
Special accessibility

Level 2

This is another element which is fun-da-men-tal for a good result. The fact is simple, it is known in trains but not well developed.

First, every passenger must embark, disembark, and walk inside the train with no stairs. Some special - comfortable, soft and large - stair could be acceptable only in the double decking, and only related to the upper deck. If absolutely necessary for the general design private stairs for each bedroom (as seen in the "Double deck, double income" idea) could be acceptable, if those stairs will be very well designed to be impeccably comfortable.

Second, every shared space, every shared passage, every shared door must be large, larger than usual train standards. Instead, private stationary spaces (i.e. bedrooms, bathrooms, showers, workrooms; apart from the previously said luxe suites) do not need to be extra sized, providing that they will always have refined high quality design and luxury touches.

Third, the entrance of bicycles is a giant problem that must be investigated and solved. Bicycles must embark/disembark/move inside easily, as human passengers. When the bicycle case is solved, also other special luggages should be satisfied in the easiness of movements (if not, it will be necessary a dedicated investigation also for them).

If all these three points will be achieved the train experience will be very satisfying, with regard to the movements chapter. This will create general satisfaction and positive reactions.

Rock train, large entrance doors and no steps to enter - BJ Liguria

Examples:

Rock train, good example because it has a comfortable access
https://it.wikipedia.org/wiki/Hitachi_Rock

Part I - The concept   Chapter 1 - Internal design

Idea 1.20
One hotel, one entrance

Level 3

Let's start with a simple observation: hotel buildings usually have one main entrance. Secundary entrances are not so important. Instead trains have entrances in each carriages; and all the entrances are equal, of the same importance. Two entrances for each carriage in the old designs, only one in some newer cases.

And... night trains? They started as trains, so here again two entrances for each carriage, or one in some newer.

So, what about our new train: it must be an hotel, more than a train. So... it could need only one main entrance for the whole train. Maybe safety rules impose entrances in each carriage; ok, but we could take them locked and open them only as emergency exits. And there is to remember that our train has all the shared spaces and passages which are larger than usual, based on the "Special accessibility" idea.

So, could we design a train where all the passengers use only one main entrance?

If yes, this would carry some advantages.

First, let's look at the carriage attendants. If I remember well, each night carriage had its own attendant. Why? To change the compartments from day layout to night layout, with those horrible hospital-like folding beds... but this does not justify one attendant for each carriage. I think (maybe wrong) that a reason for so many attendants was mainly related to safety reasons. Safety from outside. In fact, when a train stops in a station - or also along the railway somewhere for a red traffic light -

Hotel-Train, main entrance will look like this, just a little smaller - Carlos de Almeida

all the entrances of the whole train are available to... some person which is used to take things from other persons (without asking). This is a fact, we can't pretend it's not there. Are the entrances locked during the stops of the train? Yes and no. Sometimes yes, sometimes no. And in the regular stations no, the doors are not locked, they are open. So maybe carriage attendants were the defence in this (and in fact, if I remember... did those attendants look more like hotel receptionists, or like policemen?).

F. Bassi, Hotel-Train   63

So, one entrance means one attendant. With - for example - 14 carriages, we save 13 attendants. A lot of money saved.

Second, passengers would explore more spaces of the train while entering using only the main entrance; so they would have a look at a glance of the new services which are offered in our Hotel-Train, as if they were flipping through a catalogue. This could made them more interested in exploring the train later, using more services the train can offer.

Third, the main entrance could be designed as a <u>real</u> main hotel entrance, with all its importance, high design, services, receptionist, etc. This raises the quality level to that of a real hotel, moving away from the look and feel of the old trains.

Part I - The concept Chapter 1 - Internal design

Idea 1.21
One hotel, many styles

Level 3

Also here the start is a simple observation: best hotels have many different styles, in rooms and other spaces.

So, why not also in our new Hotel-Train?

For example, we have many carriages: as said at the beginning they are all-equal, ok, to reduce production, maintenance, carriage replacement and certification costs.

But could they only be the same in the main aspects, maintaining complete freedom in the surface superstructures (secundary walls, furniture, surface materials, etc.)?

If yes, some new possibility opens.

Let's imagine, each carriage could have its own personality: one carriage business-oriented, another one family-oriented, another one sporting-oriented, then shopping-oriented, art-oriented, and so on.

Naturally there will be no barrier, each passenger can walk and taste any place everywhere in the train. But the "residents" of each carriage will find their favourite environment around them, with an increase of the general satisfaction.

Another advantage of this organization is that the external communication of the different characteristics of the train will be

Hotel-Train, business-style carriage will look like this - Point3D Commercial Imaging Ltd.

Hotel-Train, sport-style carriage will look like this - tu tu

more efficacious if there are independent carriages to show, each of them with its own personality.

Hotel-Train, art-style carriage will look like this - Maria Orlova

Part I - The concept   Chapter 1 - Internal design

Idea 1.22
Natural architecture

Level 3

B ased on my personal studies and direct experience, I can affirm that natural architecture makes homes very healthy and comfortable. Much more than standard architecture do.

So, could we apply the natural architecture in our new Hotel-Train? Here natural architecture would mean to have some special concepts in several fields:

- general design;
- building materials (as said in the previous "Special materials" idea);
- furniture materials;
- textile materials;
- electrical systems (wires, plugs, wi-fi spots, etc.);
- heating and refreshing systems.

Natural architecture building - Studio FMA

I have to admit, natural architecture is practically unknown in the common public; so the competitive advantage to have something like a "natural architecture" mark, publicising it to the public, is not sure.

But what is sure is that:

- passengers would feel better, inside the train;
- the train would be "greener".

These two facts should result in a general higher satisfaction.

Chapter 2

On-board services

Idea 2.1
What about... shopping?

Level 3

Some spaces of the train can house shops, like it happens in real hotels. It is possible also to use the Modularity idea, to set and change these spaces depending on periods.

What is important is to think in advance what could be interesting to shop during the train journey. For example it could be interesting to shop the following categories:

- books (better if destination-related);
- clothes (better if destination-related);
- food (better if destination-related);
- useful objects (better if destination-related);
- toys (better if destination-related);
- souvenirs (better if destination-related);
- and many others.

In brief, any kind of item which is not too big and heavy, and that could be useful during the on-board and off-board trip, should be good; and always better if destination-related.

Hotel-Train, bookstore will look like this - Aleksandra Sapozhnikova

Fundamental requirements are:

- normal prices;
- high quality items;
- refined store design;
- a proper communication of this innovation to the off-board and on-board public.

With all that, the place should work well; and the passengers could find this activity while travelling as an original, interesting, useful experience; with a general increase of satisfaction.

There is always to remember, in fact, that the journey is long; if there is nothing to do it becomes boring. But if different activities are offered, no more boring time while travelling: everything is reversed, time becomes attractive, amusing and interesting. Passengers should want to stay inside the train, forgetting the arrival time: this is the aim.

Idea 2.2
What about... sport?

Level 3

Some spaces of the train can house gyms, like it happens in real hotels. It is possible also to use the Modularity idea, to set and change these spaces depending on periods.

Setting a gym in our new Hotel-Train should be not difficult; it needs only to think in advance what sport could be practiced. For example some doable sport could be:

- gymnastic, stretching and similar;
- yoga, pilates, and similar;
- body building;
- tiny table tennis;
- tiny basketball;
- tiny volley;
- tiny football;
- and many others.

(what I mean with "tiny"... you can imagine).

Hotel-Train, gym will look like this - Graham Mansfield

In brief, if a sport can be practiced in small spaces, it should be good. There is to note that, thanks to the Modularity idea, the size of the sport field can be adjusted on demand.

Fundamental requirements are:

- normal prices;
- high quality sport equipments;
- refined gym design;
- properly sized spaces;
- increased air renewal of the gym space;
- increased "shower time" for gym users (see the next "Universal Transport Card" idea to know more);
- a proper communication of this innovation to the off-board and on-board public.

With all that, the place should work well; and the passengers could find this activity while travelling as an original, interesting, useful experience; with a general increase of satisfaction.

There is always to remember, in fact, that the journey is long; if there is nothing to do it becomes boring. But if different activities are offered, no more boring time while travelling: everything is reversed, time becomes attractive, amusing and interesting. Passengers should want to stay inside the train, forgetting the arrival time: this is the aim.

Idea 2.3
What about... learning?

Level 3

Some spaces of the train can house school lessons, university classes and... the well-known business conferences, like it happens in real hotels. It is possible also to use the Modularity idea, to set and change these spaces depending on periods.

The thing should be interesting especially for schools: in fact, every school organises class trips; if lessons can be done during the trip, the class gains one day: vacation starts after the arrival (and the same happens on return); a result of this system is also that the school can offer more class trips.

Hotel-Train, classroom will look like this - Kenny Eliason

Universities also organise study trips sometimes; this case is similar to the said class trip of the schools.

Instead, honestly, I think and rethink... but I can't find not even a reason with which someone should arrange a moving business conference... maybe a gift-trip? A showcase-trip? I hope there could be some reason... but these cases seem so rare to me... I really can't find anything. Sorry!

In addition, there is another possibility.

The railway company itself could organise some kind of course, addressed to the train passengers; or another teacher, paying the railway company for the use of the space, could organise a personal course regarding some subject.

Passengers could be happy, sometimes, to learn something while travelling.

Fundamental requirements are:
- normal prices;
- high quality room equipments;
- refined room design;
- a proper communication of this innovation to the off-board and on-board public.

With all that, the place should work well; and the passengers could find this activity while travelling as an original, interesting, useful experience; with a general increase of satisfaction.

There is always to remember, in fact, that the journey is long; if there is nothing to do it becomes boring. But if different activities are offered, no more boring time while travelling: everything is reversed, time becomes attractive, amusing and interesting. Passengers should want to stay inside the train, forgetting the arrival time: this is the aim.

Idea 2.4
What about... tourism?

Level 3

Some spaces of the train can house touring activities, like it happens in real hotels. It is possible also to use the Modularity idea, to set and change these spaces depending on periods.

For example some touring activity could be:

- an office that gives tourist information on demand;

Hotel-Train, tourist office will look like this - Duesseldorf Tourismus

- a presentation of a certain tourist place with photo, videos, objects, explanatory panels, etc.;

- a corner to see and buy place-related touring items ("hey! this is like the already said shopping stores!" ...well, maybe yes).

There is to note that all the said things can be destination-related; but also other places can rent the train space to promote their tourist spot, even if they are in a completely different location, far from the train destination. Everything could be interesting for the train passengers!

However, if the touring space is destination-related, there is an important advantage: passengers will arrive at their destination saving a lot of time. In fact, they will already know everything they need for their visit; they no longer need to look for the local off-board tourist office, with its enormous waits and queues. And also, passengers do not need to search for tourist informations at home before departure: they will find everything they need on board the Hotel-Train, visiting the Touring Carriage. Huge amount of time saved!

Fundamental requirements are:

- normal prices;
- high quality presentations and items;
- refined space design;
- a proper communication of this innovation to the off-board and on-board public.

With all that, the place should work well; and the passengers could find this activity while travelling as an original, interesting, useful experience; with a general increase of satisfaction.

There is always to remember, in fact, that the journey is long; if there is nothing to do it becomes boring. But if different activities are offered, no more boring time while travelling: everything is reversed, time becomes attractive, amusing and interesting. Passengers should want to stay inside the train, forgetting the arrival time: this is the aim.

Idea 2.5
What about... art?

Level 3

Some spaces of the train can house art activities, like it happens in real hotels. It is possible also to use the Modularity idea, to set and change these spaces depending on periods.

For example some art activity could be:
- theatre;
- shows;
- concerts;
- art galleries;
- and many others.

Hotel-Train, art gallery will look like this - Eric Park

In brief, if an art can be presented in small spaces it should be good. There is to note that, thanks to the Modularity idea, the size of the art field can be adjusted on demand.

Fundamental requirements are:
- normal prices;
- interesting artists and art items;
- refined space design;
- a proper communication of this innovation to the off-board and on-board public.

With all that, the place should work well; and the passengers could find this activity while travelling as an original, interesting, useful experience; with a general increase of satisfaction.

There is always to remember, in fact, that the journey is long; if there is nothing to do it becomes boring. But if different activities are offered, no more boring time while travelling: everything is reversed, time becomes attractive, amusing and interesting. Passengers should want to stay inside the train, forgetting the arrival time: this is the aim.

Idea 2.6
What about... showrooms of innovative products?

Level 3

Some spaces of the train can house showroom activities, like it happens in real hotels. It is possible also to use the Modularity idea, to set and change these spaces depending on periods.

For example some showroom activity could be:

- an office that gives product information on demand;

- a presentation of the product with photos, videos, objects, explanatory panels, etc.;

- a corner to see and buy the produt itself, or product-related items ("hey! this is like the already said shopping stores! ...well, maybe yes).

Hotel-Train, showroom will look like this - Delta Light

There is to note that the things can be destination-related; but the showroom place can be rented also to promote any kind of product, even completely separated from the train destination. Everything could be interesting for the train passengers!

Fundamental requirements are:

- normal prices;
- high quality presentations and items;
- refined space design;
- really innovative and interesting products to show;
- a proper communication of this innovation to the off-board and on-board public.

With all that, the place should work well; and the passengers could find this activity while travelling as an original, interesting, useful experience; with a general increase of satisfaction.

There is always to remember, in fact, that the journey is long; if there is nothing to do it becomes boring. But if different activities are offered, no more boring time while travelling: everything is reversed, time becomes attractive, amusing and interesting. Passengers should want to stay inside the train, forgetting the arrival time: this is the aim.

Chapter 3

Off-board services

Idea 3.1
Home-To-Home Luggage Service

Level 1

This service takes the luggage from the starting home and deliveries it at the arrival home, possibly in the day of arrival of the passenger, and surely after his arrival. A refund may be offered in the event of late delivery.

This concept of service is already existing in the train's world: for example the excellent OBB company offers it.

It would undoubtedly be an useful comfort for exigent travellers; no more fatigue to move those giant and so heavy suitcases. And also it would be useful for some kind of bicycle travellers, provided that the service should be designed to manage complete bicycles as well.

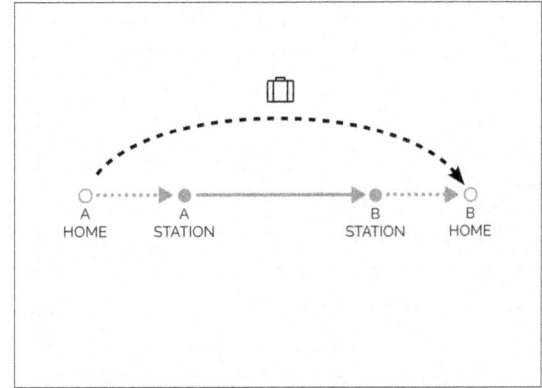

Hotel Train, Home-To-Home Luggage Service

This service will raise up the level of the railway atmosphere, taking some of the best airplane comforts (the automatic transfer of big luggages) and even increasing them at higher levels (here we are talking about home-to-home transfers, instead of airport-to-airport ones).

There is to note that this service does not eat inner train space: so it is a great alley to raise up the railway level; as said previously, we must take the most advantage of the not-eater-of-space things, because inner space is what we lack at most.

Examples:

OBB Door-to-door luggage service - bicycle included
https://www.oebb.at/en/reiseplanung-services/vor-ihrer-reise/haus-haus-gepaeck.html

Trenitalia Bagaglio Facile service - bicycle excluded
https://www.trenitalia.com/it/servizi/bagagli/bagaglio-facile.html

Idea 3.2
Home-To-HomeStation Luggage Service

Level 3

This service is completely unknown in the whole world, as far as I know. It is the said Home-To-Home Luggage Service, but with a variant: luggage is delivered at the arrival station. Luggage will travel with the Hotel-Train, and will be delivered exactly *inside* the Hotel-Train at the arrival time or earlier if requested (maximum passenger comfort, no need to look for postal offices at the station). Luggage *is not* available to passengers during the journey before delivery, with this service.

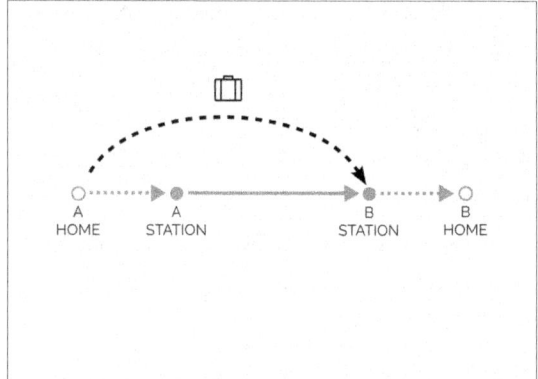

Hotel-Train, Home-To-HomeStation Luggage Service

It will be useful if passengers need, or like, to have their luggage at the arrival station.

This sometime could be the case, for example, of bicycle travellers: if, for some reason, they find complicated or dangerous to reach the departure station by bicycle, they can use this service to send bicycles directly from their departure home to the arrival station. There, they will unpack the bicycles and ride them to their final arrival home.

This service, which does not eat inner train space, will raise up the level of the railway atmosphere, taking some of the best airplane comforts and even increasing them at higher levels, as we said before.

Idea 3.3
HomeStation-To-Home Luggage Service

Level 3

This service is also completely unknown in the whole world, as far as I know. It is the exact complement of the previous Home-To-HomeStation Luggage Service: now luggage is sent from the departure station, and delivered at the final arrival home. Luggage will be sent exactly from *inside* the Hotel-Train at the departure time or later if requested (maximum passenger comfort, no need to look for postal offices at the station), and will travel with the Hotel-Train. Luggage *is not* available to passengers during the journey after dispatch, with this service.

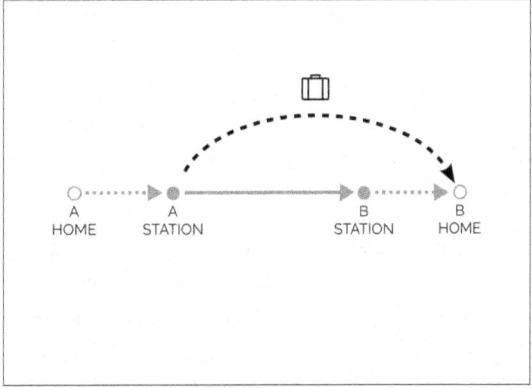

Hotel-Train, HomeStation-To-Home Luggage Service

It will be useful if passengers need, or like, to carry their luggage at the departure station.

This sometime could be the case, for example, of bicycle travellers: if, for some reason, they find complicated or dangerous to reach the final arrival home by bicycle, they can use this service to send bicycles directly from the train, at the departure station, to the final arrival home.

This service, which does not eat inner train space, will raise up the level of the railway atmosphere, taking some of the best airplane comforts and even increasing them at higher levels, as we said before.

Idea 3.4
Home-To-Station Luggage Service

Level 3

This service is a variant of the said Home-To-Home Luggage Service: this takes luggage from the starting home and deliveries it at the train departure station, surely before the train departure. Here any delay in delivery is to be avoided in any case

A similar concept of service is already existing; for example, in some important Japan stations and airports. But what I'm proposing here is considerably different, because the service should be managed by the Hotel-Train company itself; while in the Japan case, I suspect, it is always managed by separate shipping companies. So, in Japan you have to receive

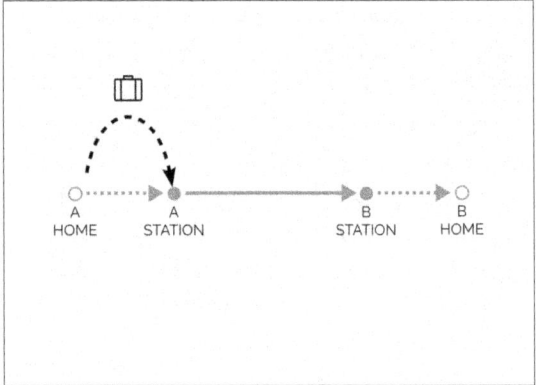

Hotel-Train, Home-To-Station Luggage Service

luggage at the shipping offices which are somewhere inside the airport/station, while in our system the train company will automatically manage luggage from home to *inside* the train, with increased comfort for passengers.

It would be useful if the passenger has some important and heavy luggage to take with it inside the train during the trip: the fatigue of luggage transfer from home to the train will be avoided; and luggage *is* available to passengers during the journey, with this service.

For example, artists and artisans might find this service useful, to better manage tools, materials and objects of their art that have to be used on the train while travelling (in the said Personal Workspace).

This service, which does not eat inner train space, will raise up the level of the railway atmosphere, taking some of the best airplane comforts and even increasing them at higher levels, as we said before.

Examples:

Luggage delivery services in Japan
https://tokyocheapo.com/travel/luggage-delivery-services/
https://www.jrailpass.com/blog/transporting-luggage-forwarding
https://www.global-yamato.com/en/hands-free-travel/facilities/tokyo_station.html
https://www.jalabc.com/en/hands-freetravel/hotel-baggage-delivery.html

Idea 3.5
Station-To-Home Luggage Service

Level 3

This service is complementary to the said Home-To-Station Luggage Service: this takes luggage from the arrival station and deliveries it at the arrival home of the passenger, possibly in the same day of the arrival. A refund may be offered in the event of late delivery.

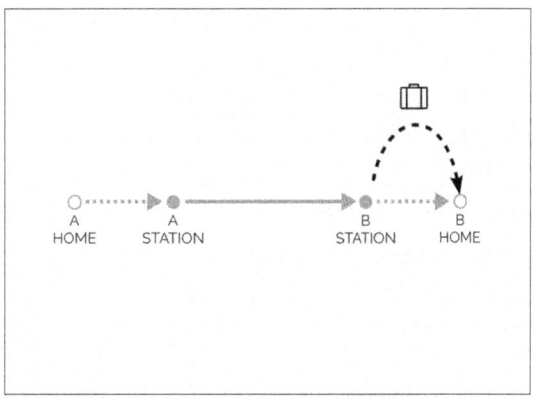

Hotel-Train, Station-To-Home Luggage Service

A similar concept of service is already existing; for example, in some important Japan stations and airports. But what I'm proposing here is considerably different, because the service should be managed by the Hotel-Train company itself; while in the Japan case, I suspect, it is always managed by separate shipping companies. So, in Japan you have to carry luggage at the shipping offices which are somewhere inside the airport/station, while in our system the train company will automatically manage luggage from *inside* the train to home, with increased comfort for passengers.

It would be useful if the passenger has some important and heavy luggage to take with it inside the train during the trip: the fatigue of luggage transfer from the train to home will be avoided; and luggage *is* available to passengers during the journey, with this service.

For example, artists and artisans might find this service useful, to better manage their tools and materials that have been used on the train while travelling (in the said Personal Workspace); even the objects of their art produced on the train can be managed with this service... and perhaps sent to the customer directly from the train: super wonderful!

This service, which does not eat inner train space, will raise up the level of the railway atmosphere, taking some of the best airplane comforts and even increasing them at higher levels, as we said before.

Examples:

Luggage delivery services in Japan
https://tokyocheapo.com/travel/luggage-delivery-services/
https://www.jrailpass.com/blog/transporting-luggage-forwarding
https://www.global-yamato.com/en/hands-free-travel/facilities/tokyo_station.html
https://www.jalabc.com/en/hands-freetravel/hotel-baggage-delivery.html

Idea 3.6
Home-To-Station Transfer Service

Level 3

This service is the same which is offered by air companies for their most expensive tickets: the company organises a dedicated transfer for the passengers and their personal luggage, from their departure home to the station.

This concept of service is probably unknown in the whole train's world (but I'm not sure... what is sure is that I've never heard about it).

It would be useful to satisfy the most exigent passengers; the fatigue of organising the transfer from home to station will be avoided.

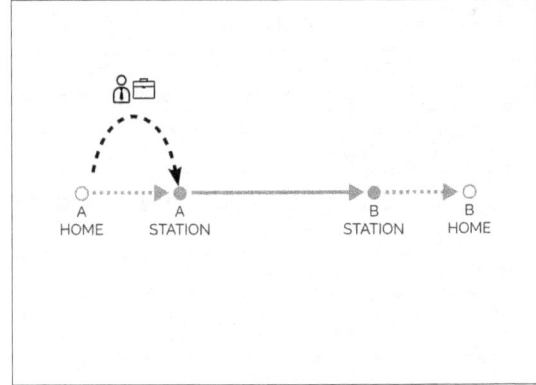

Hotel-Train, Home-To-Station Transfer Service

In the case of our Hotel-Train, I'd suggest that this service will be offered to all the passengers, not only to the most expensive tickets. This is to avoid unpleasant barriers, which often produce disappointments.

This service, which does not eat inner train space, will raise up the level of the railway atmosphere, taking some of the best airplane comforts and even increasing them at higher levels, as we said before.

Examples:

Etihad Transfer Services
https://www.etihad.com/en-it/book/airport-transfers

Idea 3.7
Station-To-Home Transfer Service

Level 3

This service is complementary to the said Home-To-Station Transfer Service: here the train company organises a dedicated transfer of passengers and their personal luggage from the arrival station to their arrival home.

This concept of service is probably unknown in the whole train's world (but I'm not sure... what is sure is that I've never heard about it).

It would be useful to satisfy the most exigent passengers; the fatigue of organising the transfer from station to home will be avoided.

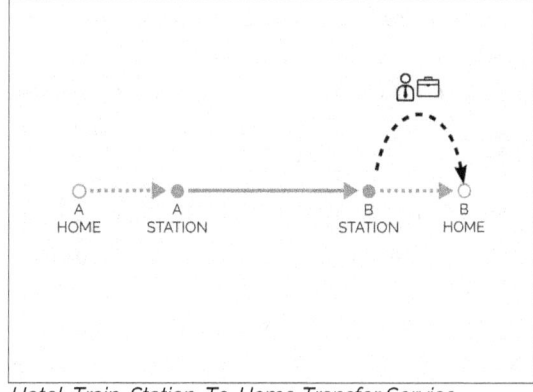

Hotel-Train, Station-To-Home Transfer Service

In the case of our Hotel-Train, I'd suggest that this service will be offered to all the passengers, not only to the most expensive tickets. This is to avoid unpleasant barriers, which often produce disappointments.

This service, which does not eat inner train space, will raise up the level of the railway atmosphere, taking some of the best airplane comforts and even increasing them at higher levels, as we said before.

Examples:

Etihad Transfer Services
https://www.etihad.com/en-it/book/airport-transfers

Idea 3.8
Residential Station Lounge

Level 3

This service is similar to what is offered by air companies, and by some train companies too, for their most expensive tickets: the company organises a dedicated lounge inside the station for the most comfortable stay of passengers before departure and after arrival.

Here I'd propose some innovation, though: this lounge should be more "residential-oriented". I mean, not only a big hall with armchairs, sofas and shared working areas; but with some of the well-known Personal Workspaces added. In addition, it will be dedicated to all the passengers (not only to the most expensive tickets); because barriers, as said, produce disappointments.

This concept of service is probably expensive for a new train company and could be delayed to later periods.

It would be useful to satisfy the most exigent passengers; the station becomes like a residential office, for them.

This service, which does not eat inner train space, will raise up the level of the railway atmosphere, taking some of the best airplane comforts and even increasing them at higher levels, as we said before.

Hotel-Train, Residential Station Lounge will look like this - Dillon Shook

Examples:

Etihad Airport Lounges
https://www.etihad.com/en-it/fly-etihad/lounges

Trenitalia Freccia Lounge, for the businessmen
https://www.trenitalia.com/it/servizi/in-stazione/sale-alta-velocita/freccialounge.html

Trenitalia Freccia Club, for the poor man of businessmen
https://www.trenitalia.com/it/servizi/in-stazione/sale-alta-velocita/frecciaclub.html

Idea 3.9
Residential Transfer Lounge

Level 3

This service is completely unknown in all the world, I think. Basically, there would be the said Home-To-Station and Station-To-Home transfers organised by the company, but in this case these services would use a special vehicle, a special big bus containing... the well-known Personal Workspaces.

In this case the bus will take different passengers in the same trip; i.e. the bus will be not be dedicated to one passenger only. And obviously, the bus should be... "double-decked".

This concept of service is probably expensive for a new train company and could be delayed to later periods. It could seem also difficult to realise, because of the novelty of a similar impossible "office-bus" object... but, in reality, special nightliner buses already exist, so it could be thinkable to design and build a special "workliner" bus. Investigation needed.

Hotel-Train, Residential Transfer Lounge in the Personal Workspace variant will look like this - eila.de

It would be useful to satisfy the most exigent passengers; the transfer to and from the station sometimes could be long, and in this case even that time is useful to work as the passenger were in a real office.

An interesting variant could be a special bus which will be not work-oriented, but relax-oriented: basically it should be designed internally like one of the current lounge rooms which are in the airports or in the stations (currently dedicated to the most

Hotel-Train, Residential Transfer Lounge in the relax variant will look like this - Mark Chaves

expensive tickets). This could be better, if the transfer time will be not long, around 30-60 minutes for example. Investigation needed here too.

This service, which does not eat inner train space, will raise up the level of the railway atmosphere, taking some of the best airplane comforts and even increasing them at higher levels, as we said before.

Examples:

Clemens Behle nightliner double-deck buses
https://www.setra-bus.com/en_DE/brand/setraworld-magazine/touring-with-rockstars.html

Zeppelin nightliner double-deck bus
https://www.youtube.com/watch?v=vSSmKtd5R7s

Wendt nightliner single-deck 9-seats bus
https://tourbussewendt.de/nightliner/

Eila nightliner double-deck bus
https://www.eila.de/de/mietpark/premium-nightliner-245/

Chapter 4

Economics

Idea 4.1
Different passenger, different strategy

Level 3

The initial question here is: what type of passengers could our train attract, in theory? Let's try to write a list, based on what was said in previous ideas, grouping here in categories:

- "business": businessmen, remote workers, researchers;
- "art": painters, writers, pro readers, sculptors-maybe, musicians, singers, music composers, video and film makers, photographers, directors, actors, artisans, art observers, inventors, dreamers, and others;
- "cinema": cinephiles ("hey! it's art too!" - yes, but it needs a separate carriage to set the cine space);
- "academy": teachers, learners and students;
- "sport": sporting enthusiasts and pro;
- "shopping": shopping and showroom enthusiasts and pro;
- "touring": touring enthusiasts and pro;
- "family": families;
- "bicycle": bicycle travellers and passengers with special luggages;
- "luxe": luxury enthusiasts;
- ok, now I stop here... others maybe.

This is a lot of categories... hopefully enough to make our Hotel-Train full all year long.

But now, the fact is: how can we do to attract all these categories at best?

Well, first of all remembering the "One hotel, many styles" idea, each carriage could be dedicated to one of these categories.

More exactly, maybe some category (as business, for example) could require more than one carriage, to satisfy the transport demand of that category at best: investigation needed. And maybe, also, a whole carriage could be too large

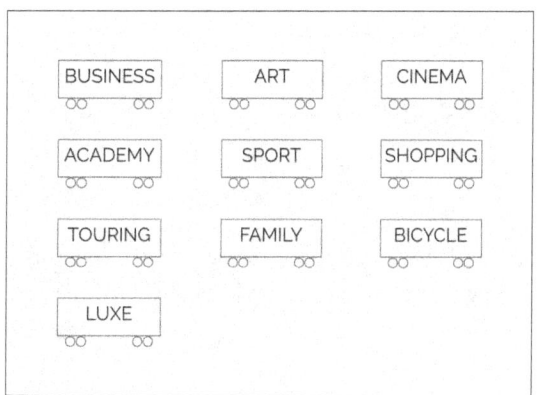

Hotel-Train, types of passengers and carriages

to house the demand of some other category, which in this case will be mixed with another category using the said Modularity idea.

At the end of the speech, simply, the composition of the train - regarding the said carriage categories offered - will vary during the year; for example, if we have a total of 14 carriages, in some periods like Autumn the carriages (always all-equal in the basic structure, as said) could be internally arranged and externally presented as:

- 5 "business" carriages;
- 1 "cinema" carriage;
- 1 "art" carriage;
- 1 "academy" carriage;
- 2 "sport" carriages;
- 1 "shopping" carriage;
- 1 "family" carriage
- 1 "touring" + "bicycle" carriage;
- 1 "luxe" carriage.

while in other periods like Summer it could be:

- 1 "business" carriages;
- 1 "cinema" carriage;
- 2 "art" carriage;
- 2 "academy" carriage;
- 3 "sport" carriages;
- 1 "shopping" carriage;
- 1 "touring" carriage;
- 1 "family" carriage;
- 1 "bicycle" carriage;
- 1 "luxe" carriage.

And there is to add a second fact: obviously, each category of passengers will require its proper communication, to be informed about what the new Hotel-Train could offer to them.

Idea 4.2
Different passenger, infinite fares

Level 3

And... what about the fares? Yes, there will be a huge amount of different fares, because each carriage type (as said in the previous "Different passenger, different strategy" idea) will have its own characteristics and services - which means different costs and so different fares - and in addition each carriage will offer different types of bedroom (single, twin, cheap-luxe, top-of-the-top-luxe, for example).

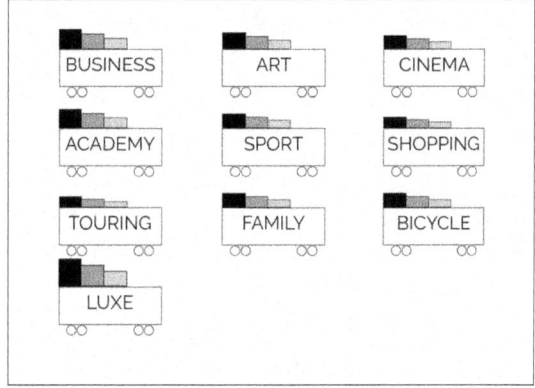

Hotel-Train, different fares in each carriage type

So there will be infinite fares, many more than a couple of classes as in ordinary trains; in our new Hotel-Train there will be the selection of carriage type/bedroom type which will provide the right price; and all this will vary also during the days of booking, if our train will follow the well-known dynamic pricing system used by the air and rail companies... investigation needed here. And there will be also quantity discounts, season tickets, on-board services fares, etc...

Idea 4.3
Universal Transport Card

Level 3

But... so... will the passengers lose their heads inside the said mass of infinite fares, while they are buying the various tickets and services? No, because they will use the "Universal Transport Card" which:

- makes the ticketing so easy to be practically invisible;

- opens all the doors on board, one-key-for-all;

- makes the seasonal ticketing automatic, a posteriori, with no hassle;

- and also makes the passengers happy!

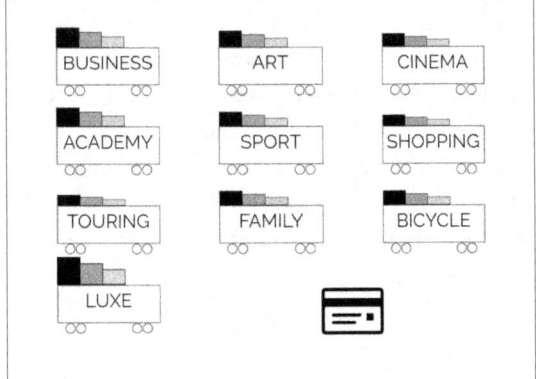

Hotel-Train, Universal Transport Card makes ticketing easier, opens all the doors on board and makes seasonal ticketing automatic a posteriori

Let's imagine: a card, linked to a certain amount of money (for example, prepaid). There is a name linked to the card, this name is useful in case the card is lost; but the card can be used by anyone, even without giving the exact passenger name, so that privacy is respected. I set the journey, my favourite carriage type ("Sport"), my favourite bedroom type ("Top-luxe"); I see the price: too high; I change the bedroom to the "Single": oh, this is better; I click "Buy". Done, finished - no other passages to do. From now on the ticket exists in the system and it is linked to the card. So I go to the train at the departure time taking no paper tickets - those odious pieces of paper that are always cumbersome and heavy and even faded. I take only the card in my wallet, open the doors with the card and go to my single bedroom to settle the luggage. Then I go to the gym: the card opens the gym also, its use was already included in my ticket because I chose the "Sport" carriage type. A bit of fitness exercise, and then return to my bedroom to take a shower. The shower time is limited automatically by the card ("...hey, we are in a hotel!" - Yes, but also the Etihad The Residence limited the shower time). I read the time in the shower screen and take the shower comfortably because the available time is long. The shower is not large but of spa-level, so very very pleasant. Then I take a walk outside, heading to the three-stars "the Fork" restaurant, few carriages ahead. I have the card with me, lock the door... and so on.

And even more: the next month I have to take another journey. I repeat the previous passages with the same card. This time I choose the "Cheap-luxe" bedroom type. I go to the train, etc. Then I repeat the same for another journey, and for another one, and another one. At this point I realise: oh, what a pity... I forgot there was the seasonal ticket, I could take it at the first trip saving money... I am a sad passenger. But no, instead I am not! The card system took track of all the tickets which have been purchased in the past, so that all the fares - even the past ones, already payed - are automatically converted to the most convenient seasonal ticket fare, because I buyed a lot of journeys. So this trip is free and I am very happy. Wonderful!

Idea 4.4
Universal Transport Card on-board payments

Level 3

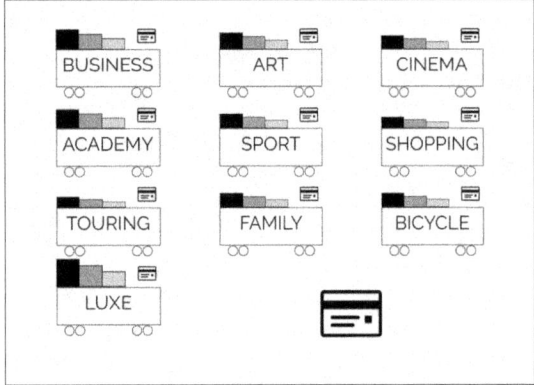

The Universal Transport Card (UTC) will be useful also because it can be conveniently used on board, to pay any optional service the Hotel-Train offers during the trip. In this way there is no need to manage money on board, so everything is easier for the passenger and even the railway company saves money (no safety issue if there is no money inside the train; but it is to remember that there are, as in all payment cards, informatic safety issues to consider).

Hotel-Train, Universal Transport Card is used in all the payments on board

This can happen if UTC will be the only way to buy the ticket. Now, in this way some passengers could find obstacles in buying the ticket, if they are beginners and know nothing in advance about the UTC system… but these cases can be managed too: simply those passengers will buy a new UTC recharging it with some money; if they are exitant in giving a big amount of money at the beginning no problem, they can recharge also while they will be on board during the trip (maybe with a little surcharge due to this on-board money management).

Chapter 5

Routes & Timetables

Part I - The concept   Chapter 5 - Routes & Timetables

Idea 5.1
Undulatory Paths

Level 3

The usual routes of night trains go from A to B, where A and B are big main towns, using the straightest line possible. Some stops between A and B are possible only if there are some important towns along that straight AB line. If the transport demand from A to B, middle towns included, is enough to make the train full all-year-long ok, this is a good organisation for the first period of a starting railway company.

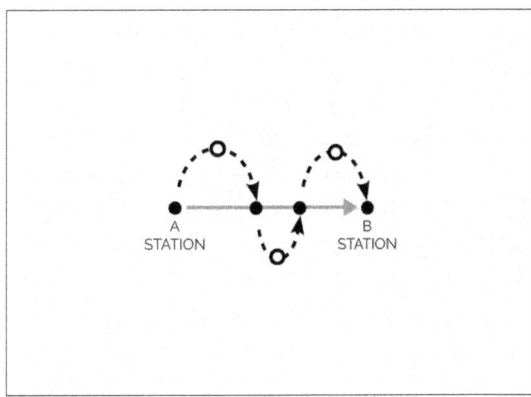

Hotel-Train, Undulatory Path

But... what happens if the demand from A to B, middle towns included, will be not enough?

The night train fails; or the train must find some new way. Now, a new way could be this: offer an "Undulatory Path" route, which follows an undulatory line instead of a straight line, and which is designed exactly to reach and stop also in many other towns, large or small, besides A and B.

"Hey! The trip time will become longer!"

Yes, but we are having dinner in the famous three-stars "the Fork" restaurant, taking a stellar shower and exercising in the gym, the exact time doesn't matter.

Undulatory Paths can increase the Hotel-Train audience to the maximum imaginable, if they will be well designed.

Idea 5.2
Circular Paths

Level 3

The usual routes of night trains go from A to B, where A and B are big main towns, using the straightest line possible. Some stops between A and B are possible only if there are some important towns along that straight AB line. If the transport demand from A to B, middle towns included, is enough to make the train full all-year-long ok, this is a good organisation for the first period of a starting railway company.

But... what happens if the demand from A to B, middle towns included, will be not enough?

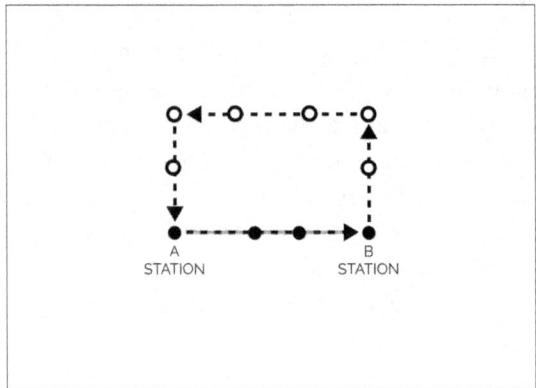

Hotel-Train, Circular Path

The night train fails; or the train must find some new way. Now, a new way could be this: offer a "Circular Path" route, which follows a circular line instead of a straight line, and which is designed exactly to reach and stop also in many other important towns in addition to A and B.

There is to note that a circular route is not a mere increase in the number of stops, because it offers a novelty: the fact that from each station you can reach - without changing trains - any other station of an entire territory, and not only the stations which are along one straight band. This increases the flexibility of the railway mode, which was traditionally quite rigid, approaching automotive levels of flexibility.

> "Hey! This way there is not a real start of the train anymore, there is not a real end... it's a mixture, a jam, a marmalade where any station can be a start, any station can be an end, and all that could be at any time of night and day!"

Yes, but c'mon, we are a modern high quality hotel, guests can check-in also at 2 a.m. and check-out at midnight if they like to.

> "Hey! The trip time will become longer!"

Yes, but we are having dinner in the famous three-stars "the Fork" restaurant, taking a stellar shower and exercising in the gym, the exact time doesn't matter.

Circular Paths can increase the Hotel-Train audience to the maximum imaginable, if they will be well designed. And... could they be combined with the well-known Undulatory Paths? Yes, certainly...

Idea 5.3
Undulatory&Circular Paths

Level 3

The usual routes of night trains go from A to B, where A and B are big main towns, using the straightest line possible. Some stops between A and B are possible only if there are some important towns along that straight AB line. If the transport demand from A to B, middle towns included, is enough to make the train full all-year-long ok, this is a good organisation for the first period of a starting railway company.

But... what happens if the demand from A to B, middle towns included, will be not enough?

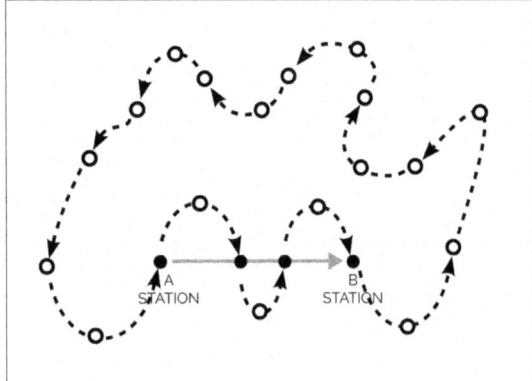

Hotel-Train, Undulatory&Circular Path

The night train fails; or the train must find some new way. Now, a new way could be this: offer an "Undulatory&Circular Path" route, which is a mix of the said Undulatory Path and Circular Path. It's so simple!

Idea 5.4
Low Speed

Level 3

The usual night trains go at the usual train speed (or maybe even at the maximum speed possibile, I don't know). But, as said, we are in the best refined hotel of the world, speed and time do not matter. So our new Hotel-Train could proceed also at a very low speed, compared to the ordinary trains.

This could carry some advantages:

- less noise;
- less vibrations;
- less accelerations and decelerations;
- less fatigue and maintenance in carriages;
- less expense of energy;
- more comfort for passengers;
- nicer, calmer views from the windows and from the said "Panoramic points" of the train.

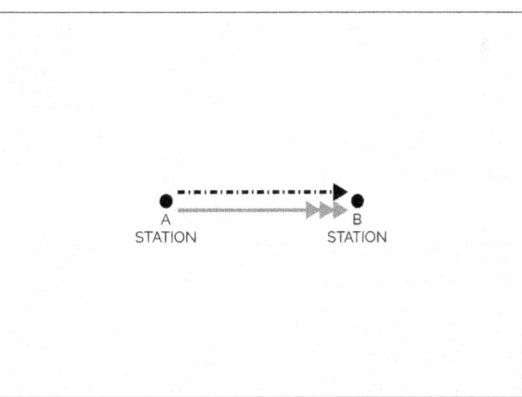

Hotel-Train, Low Speed

Certainly, it is necessary that the speed is kept above a fair limit, to take the total trip time at an acceptable level; this depends on the different routes and cases - investigation needed.

Idea 5.5
Day Use

Level 3

The usual night trains travel during the evening, the night, the morning. But we are an hotel, and lastly the hotels experienced that giving the rooms also for "Day Use" is often profitable. So, the conclusion is simple: our new night train will offer also day routes, in which passengers will find all the night services of our train, complete bedrooms included, but travelling during the day.

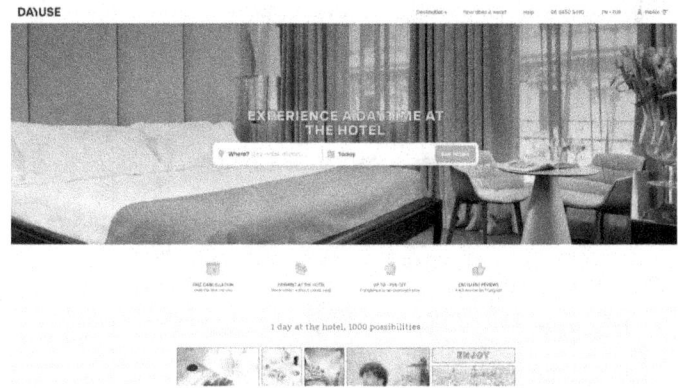

Hotel-Train, Day Use will look like this - dayuse.com

If the Hotel-Train will run during both night and day it will be really exploited to the maximum.

"Hey! But when the bedrooms will be set, if the train always run?"

We are an hotel, there are not "running time" and "stopping time", there is only "time": the rooms will be set as it happens in all the hotels, when there is the right time. Also during run.

There is also to consider a fact. I don't know exactly, but I suspect that many people might be afraid to travel by train during night. In the plane it doesn't matter, because sky is sky and day/night no longer make sense there. But along a railway... which is like a street... with terrestrial objects and environments... I suspect that many people could prefer to see what is around them, while they are travelling. So, these people would be very very happy to find our hotel-on-railway for Day Use... the trip here will be so much more interesting compared to the ordinary day trains, bullet ones included.

So here again, the Day Use could expand the audience of our new train to a much higher level. And in addition the carriages, if they will be used also during the day, will be utilised more efficiently; so that the costs will be more easily amortised. Perhaps with the systems we are going to see here in the following...

Only one train instead of two, 50% cost cut, with Day Use

This is an interesting aspect, regarding the Day Use: with this system, the return train could be avoided. I mean: in the usual straight path, with a night train running from A to B, it is necessary to have also a second night train running at the same time from B to A; this, to satisfy both the AB and BA transport demands in all the days. But, let's imagine if I have only one train which does the following:

- starts from A in the evening and arrives in B in the next morning;
- then starts from B in the same morning (with the Day Use) and returns to A in that afternoon;
- then starts again from A in that evening, and so on.

This way offers both the AB and BA trips in all the days, using only one train. The AB demand is satisfied with overnight trips, and the BA demand with daytime trips. We are a complete hotel with Personal Workspaces and all the other special on-board services, restaurants and amenities: it means that also the daytime journey is a useful and pleasant time, it is never a waste of time.

Having only one train would mean cutting costs by around 50%, compared to the case with two trains. An advantage that is not small.

However, this system will not satisfy the demand of passengers who want to go and come back without having nights to stay out (apart from the nights in the Hotel-Train); I mean, this type of passengers would want to do the following journey:

- departure from A in the evening;
- arrival in B in the next morning;
- all the day in B for work, tourism or other;
- then in *the same evening* departure from B;
- final return in A the next morning.

They are not satisfied because the first Hotel-Train, for them, leaves B in the morning of the next day, and not in the same evening. So those passengers have to stay one night in a hotel in B. If the night stay in B is managed automatically by the Hotel-Train company, to make things easier, it may be good... in any case there is to investigate if the said 50% cost cut balances the missing or disappointed passengers of this type.

Only one train instead of two, 50% cost cut, with Day Use and Circular Path

If we take the previous system adding the said Circular Path, our train:

- starts from A in the evening and arrives in B in the next morning;
- then starts from B in the same morning (with the Day Use) and stops in C in that midday;
- then starts from C in the same midday and returns to A in that afternoon;
- then starts again from A in the evening, and so on.

This way also offers both the AB (overnight) and BA (daytime) trips in all the days, using only one train; but now there is the addition that the same train reaches also C, following the A-B-C-A Circular Path in a continuous, endless, head-spinning, loop.

At a first sight adding a circular path as said here (A-B-C-A) could be more efficient and "revolutionary", because it also allows C to be reached with the same train, without changes (C is just a symbol, it can mean in reality a whole group of separate stations, all with their citizens departing or arriving). Investigation necessary.

Two trains, 100% revenue increase, with Day Use

If we prefer to have two trains, to satisfy both the AB and BA night travel demands, the Day Use allows us to double the number of available departures. In fact the train T_1 in a certain day would do the following:

- starts from A in the evening and arrives in B in the next morning;
- then starts from B in the same morning (with the Day Use) and returns to A in that afternoon;
- then starts again from A in that evening, and so on.

And the train T_2 in the same day would do the following:

- starts from B in the evening and arrives in A in the next morning;
- then starts from A in the same morning (with the Day Use) and returns to B in that afternoon;
- then starts again from B in that evening, and so on.

This way offers two departures from A to B in each day (in the evening with overnight trip and in the morning with daytime trip), and the same applies for the departures from B to A (two departures per day, in the evening and in the morning).

If we are so successful that we have all the trips roughly full, we obtain a 100% increase of revenues compared to the standard night-use-only of the same two trains. An advantage that is not small.

Two trains, 100% revenue increase, with Day Use and Circular Path

The previous system with two trains can be obviously improved adding the well-known Circular Path. The train T_1 now does the following:

- starts from A in the evening and arrives in B in the next morning;
- then starts from B in the same morning (with the Day Use) and stops in C in that midday;
- then starts from C in the same midday and returns to A in that afternoon;
- then starts again from A in that evening, and so on.

And the train T_2 in the same period does the following:

- starts from B in the evening and arrives in A in the next morning;
- then starts from A in the same morning (with the Day Use) and stops in C in that midday;

- then starts from C in the same midday and returns to B in that afternoon;
- then starts again from B in that evening, and so on.

This really seems to be the maximum imaginable utilisation of our two trains. We obtain all the stations A, B, C with two departures (and arrivals) per day. And remember that C is just a symbol, it can mean in reality a whole group of separate stations, all with their citizens departing or arriving.

Furthermore, having two trains with this system allows all AB and BA journeys to be made without increasing any journey time (in contrast, a simple circular route with only one train usually has a certain A-B outward journey time and a longer B-C-A return journey time).

I can't imagine more than this!

Examples:

Day Use in standard hotels
https://www.mews.com/en/blog/day-use-hotel-rooms

Idea 5.6
Forgotten Stations

Level 3

The usual night trains connect main towns only. This is probably in order not to waste resources, concentrating only on the most profitable spots.

But remember, we have some new possibility around here: the said Undulatory Path, Circular Path, Day Use... and also all the previous ideas said in other chapters; each of them contributes to increasing the audience of the Hotel-Train. With all these expansion concepts, it seems possible, at a first sight, to consider also some minor stations and serve them, some of those stations that are forgotten by all but little regional trains. Because the fact is that sometimes, or even often, there are very interesting spots close to some of those "Forgotten Stations"; interesting for touring aims (and anyone takes a trip for tourism sometime) but also for business, culture, etc. So people should be interested in using those stations too; if the company can afford the hazard (hoping to have the train full in any case, thanks to the said new ideas) it should be advisable to open this new market, "big night hotel trains in forgotten stations". This new market, if it will be confirmed that it exists in reality and not only in theory, will contribute to expand the train business.

Hotel-Train, Forgotten Station will look like this - Michele Brina

Examples:

Castagno station
https://it.wikipedia.org/wiki/Stazione_di_Castagno

Idea 5.7
On Demand Stations

Level 3

The usual night trains have fixed stops only. When there is a stop on the route, the train stops always.

But what about the possibility of having "On Demand Stations"? They are currently used in some regional railways, but not for long distance trains (as far as I know). It seems to me that On Demand Stations could be useful for the Hotel-Train, in order to expand the area served by the train without losing resources when there are no passengers. If no passenger books a departure or an arrival in a station, stopping there is useless and wastes energy and time. This is valid - and even probably necessary - for the said minor Forgotten Stations; but maybe sometimes it could be valid also for some bigger stops.

However there is to consider the balance with the very-last-minute passengers that could like to buy the ticket at the very last moment, maybe directly at the departure station, few time before departure: if this behaviour is allowed in a station, that station cannot be on-demand; otherwise there is a risk of losing some passenger at the station when the train passes without stopping.

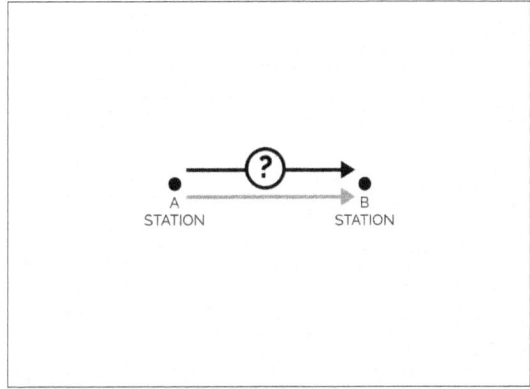
Hotel-Train, On Demand Station

Hotel-Train, On Demand Station will look like this - Emilio2005

But the fact is: will the very-last-minute behaviour be allowed or not, in our new train? I suspect that the whole organization with very-last-minute passengers would be impossible for a real Hotel-Train, even in a major station and not only in the minor forgotten ones; anyway... investigation needed.

So, apart from the very-last-minute matter, if the railway network rules will allow the On Demand Stations it could be advisable to be flexible at most and design this kind of stop wherever possible.

Examples:

Settequerce/Siebenheich station
https://suedtirol.live/it/negozio/stazione-ferroviaria-settequerce-settequerce-p56705
https://it.wikipedia.org/wiki/Stazione_di_Settequerce

Idea 5.8
On Demand Routes

Level 3

The usual night trains have fixed routes only. The train follows always that route.

But, after having introduced the possibility of the said On Demand Stations, it comes automatically to theorise also the "On Demand Routes": i.e., routes which can be modified depending on the various bookings which have been received.

Also in this case there is the very-last-minute passenger matter to consider, as said previously.

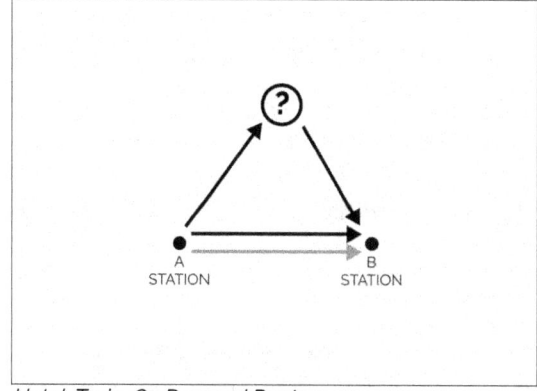

Hotel-Train, On Demand Route

The On Demand Routes, if allowed by the railway network rules, would expand the flexibility at most. Certainly the complexity of the management also would increase at most, and could become so complicated to make this way impossible or not profitable. Investigation needed.

Idea 5.9
Stable Stations

Level 3

The usual night trains allow passengers to stay inside the train only during the running time. The train stops only few time in a station, then proceeds to the next one. And so on.

But as said before we are an hotel, so we have no "running time" and "stopping time", we have only "time". An hotel does not refuse a guest because it is not during a sort of "running time". And so... why not design some stops that are "Stable Stations", I mean with the train stably fixed in that stop for a long time - i.e. one day, one day and one night, or more - and with indoor passengers included?

This could increase the satisfaction of passengers.

In fact, for example, let's suppose that a businessman has to stay in a town for one day, from the morning to the evening. All right, he arrives in that town with our train in the morning, leaves the train and go for business. And in the evening he will take our train again to return home. But during the day that businessman has no point of support in the city: and so what about the luggage with clothes, refreshing items, showers, bathrooms... certainly it is doable, but only if things are light, and in any case the comfort is not the maximum... or certainly he could book a "day use" hotel to stay comfortably, but in this case there would be the transfers from the train to the hotel and viceversa - check-in check-out included - which take resources.

Hotel-Train, Stable Station will look like this - Velvet

Instead, let's imagine if the bedroom inside the train (Hotel-Train) remains the bedroom of the businessman also during all the day. That bedroom is his home: he can go in and out whenever he likes, luggages and refreshings stay inside that bedroom during all the time. The experience in town would be completely new, much more comfortable.

And the same is valid for touring passengers, even more: they are always loaded with complicated cameras, clothes for all the weathers, bottles of water, guidebooks... the backpack here is much more heavy than a simple business briefcase.

Obviously there is a problem to solve. Will the station allow the train to stay inside for a long time? If yes, at what price?

I suspect all this could be impossible in the main stops, but maybe possible in some minor Forgotten Station. Investigation needed.

Idea 5.10
Personal Stable Stations

Level 3

This is the solution in case it is impossible to have the said Stable Station in some important location: build a "Personal Stable Station" exactly for the Hotel-Train in that location.

I admit, this is a very cloudy idea. Almost impossible to realise. But this is not 100% sure, maybe with some strange happening resources could arrive from somewhere, and so... the idea is here.

It should work well: the Hotel-Train arrives in its Personal Stable Station (which is a land with personal railway track and few well-designed off-board services); stays there stably for a day and/or night (even more days/nights, depending on cases) and then goes. The Hotel-Train, while it stays there, is the stable home of the passengers; they can walk outside around having their residential home in the same bedroom they have during the running trip.

What is difficult is also to find an available land close to the interesting location. But maybe it could be possible in some case.

Hotel-Train, Personal Stable Station will look like this - Neil Mewes

Idea 5.11

Railway Cruises

Level 2

The usual night trains follow a route with the only aim to carry passengers from A to B. Everything in between is useless.

But we have a real hotel with refined sevices inside. And we have seen a lot of new strange but quite interesting concepts...

- Undulatory Paths;
- Circular Paths;
- Low speed;
- Day Use;
- Forgotten Station;
- Stable Station...

What happens if we take all these concepts and mix them together? It appears a "Railway Cruise"!

"Hey... we said we wanted only a business hotel train!"

Yes, but in some period it could be used for a cruise, couldn't it? For example, during usual vacation periods.

Hotel-Train, Railway Cruise will look like this - The Luxury Train Club

Well, I have to admit. I thought I was the first, years ago, to have imagined the possibility of real railway cruises... but I was wrong. First of all I realised I already watched a tv series with a train cruise when I was a child (even if I forgot it later: Supertrain). But even because others already thought this concept of travelling: luxury trains already do exactly that, and I don't know since when.

Anyway no problem, the experience of a real railway cruise could be very pleasant and would transform our Hotel-Train in a luxury cruise ship. On-board services are already available, as said all across this dream-project; it would need only a proper design of the route - and here the possibilities across the different European countries are surely unlimited and breathtaking.

Examples:

Supertrain TV drama - it was this that opened my mind!
https://en.wikipedia.org/wiki/Supertrain
http://nbc_supertrain.tripod.com/

The Luxury Train Club - an impressive list of astonishing train cruises
https://www.luxurytrainclub.com/

Goldean Eagle - another impressive list of astonishing train cruises
https://www.goldeneagleluxurytrains.com/

Part II - The train

Here each idea, which has been showed in the previous part, is used like a brick; combining all the bricks together, the new Hotel-Train is built (in a first, theoretical, form).

Chapter 6

Layout design

Idea 6.1
Business Carriage

Level 3

After having dreamed a new Hotel-Train in all the previous chapters, now is the time to become a real designer and pull out some drawings, at a first raw level. This is very important to verify better the (theorical) possibilities of the previous dreams, to see if some change is needed somewhere, and... to imagine the future train experience.

Let's start from the first type: "Business Carriage".

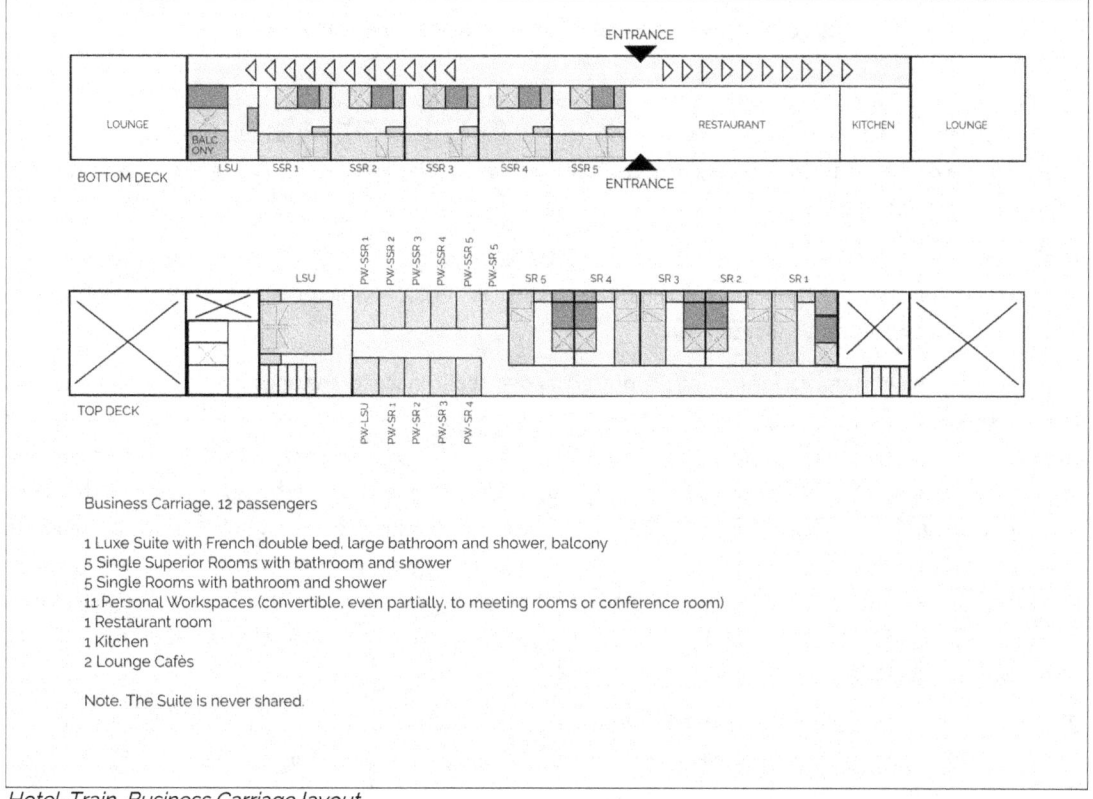

Hotel-Train, Business Carriage layout

"...hey! Why you put a Level 3, the idea of a business-type carriage is not yours but the company's!"

Yes, it was the new railway company - with which I am collaborating, in my imagination though - which had the basic starting concept: a business-hotel-style night train. But I put the Level 3 because I'm proposing here my own layout design, with my unique concept of Personal Workspaces and my own positioning and designing of all the rooms, restaurant and cafés.

This Business Carriage is the base layout from which all the other carriages are derivated, with only few modifications, as we'll see in the following paragraphs. So we'll have basically all-equal carriages with few modifications obtained using the well-known, already said, Modularity idea. This base layout, as well as all its variants, contains exactly all the ideas said before in the previous "Internal design", "On-board services" and "Economics" chapters - none excluded. The remaining "Off-boards services" and "Routes & Timetables" chapters also apply here, but they deal more with off-board aspects of the train.

Here in the Business Carriage all the rooms are single, because we are in business. Only exception is the suite, but it can be booked also by single passengers to have more comfort and space (maybe paying a little less than two passengers... investigation needed).

Now let's take a closer look at the different spaces in the carriage.

Entrances, inclined passages and the "quasi-impossible mission"

The figure shows the position of both the entrances of the carriage (left and right side); they are placed at the lowest level of the carriage, to be at the same level of the station platforms, similarly to the layout of the aforementioned "Rock" train. These entrances will usually only be used as emergency exits, as said in the "One hotel, one entrance" idea.

In the entrance at the top of the picture, that is on the corridor side, there are two inclined passages (15% slope) that go along the corridor, to the right and to the left. These inclined passages have to climb around 90 cm, so they need around 6 meters each.

There will be some complications on the top deck, above these inclined passages: the top deck must have some "indentations" in its design (even hidden below some furniture, wherever possible) to accommodate the inclined passage underneath; for this reason, some rooms of the top deck - unfortunately, suite included - will have a reduced internal height (up to a little more than 180 cm) and/or a higher position of the lower bed (up to about 60 cm). Some steps will also be necessary inside some rooms on the bottom deck; and here, I am only just realising this now, rooms SSR2 and SSR3 of the figure could be mirrored left-right, to avoid or reduce their steps. It must also be said that the corridor of the bottom deck could have a little indentation in its ceiling, on its bottom side in figure, to give more available height to the rooms above it. All this requires a finer investigation.

This design seems to solve the "quasi-impossible mission" that was introduced in the "Double-deck, double corridor" idea, at the beginning of this book. In fact in this design we have, as we were looking for, a double-deck carriage, with two corridors, without stairs in the corridor of the bottom deck.

Luxe Suite

The "Luxe Suite" has the entrance at the lower deck, without stairs from the corridor here; at this level it features a large spa bathroom with large shower, and a private balcony to observe outdoor views in a new astonishing way. At this level there is also a wardrobe for hanging clothes.

The balcony, as all the balconies in this train (there will be others!), could be not completely open as in the stable buildings; here we are in a moving train, so maybe it is better to provide a "kneeling" wrought-iron grating that keeps plants and flowers inside, in a very pleasant view, and avoids danger to passengers in the event of sudden shocks of the train.

The suite then has its own staircase, large and soft, comfortable, leading to the upstairs sleeping area. Here we find a French double bed, with bedside tables, and top-notch amenities like in the best hotel luxury suites.

There aren't tickets for shared use of suites, double or twin rooms. This is because, firstly, we are a hotel; and secondly, because the shared use of a room may in some cases leave a passenger with a certain unpleasant memory, whereas our new Hotel-Train should produce only beautiful memories in passengers.

Single Superior Rooms

The lower deck also houses five "Single Superior Rooms". They are called Superior because they are a little larger than the other standard rooms. All the Superior Rooms provide a bathroom with shower, not large but refined like a spa so that it should result very pleasant, and a wardrobe. All beds have a bedside table and all the fine amenities we can imagine, as in the off-board high-end hotel rooms.

Restaurant, Lounge and Staff

On the lower deck of the carriage there is a well-refined restaurant with dining room, as well as two lounge and café areas. The kitchen is located nearby.

In each carriage, a staff of at least two persons (chef and waiter) is required for the restaurant and lounges. Where this staff sleep? In the restaurant: this is a completely separated space and will have a proper convertible area which will transform in bedroom after the closing time and will disappear within the opening time. The restaurant must have also one bathroom (not shown in figure), usable by both guests and staff.

In case of necessity, the staff can check the use of the previously said entrances of the carriage.

Single Rooms

From the lounge at the right end of the carriage a large and soft, comfortable, staircase leads upstairs to the upper deck. Here we have five standard "Single Rooms", which are like the Superior Rooms but only a little smaller.

Personal Workspaces

The upper deck then contains the said innovative Personal Workspaces, one for each room of the carriage. The Personal Workspaces are the small (tiny) offices where each passenger can concentrate and work.

"...hey! They are too tiny!"

Yes they are tiny, in this layout, but I think still very useful if well internally designed and refined. Anyway their right size has to be investigated and experimented.

Service Space

As said previously, the area which houses the Personal Workspaces is in reality a whole open space, which can be set with different layouts upon request. So it is possible to collect more Personal Workspaces to have a meeting room, for example; or it is also possible to have all the open area to set a large conference room. This area will be called "Service Space" in the following.

Idea 6.2
Art Carriage

Level 3

The "Art Carriage" is exactly like the said Business Carriage, with the only difference that all the single rooms, except one, here are twin rooms (using bunk beds). I said except one because the first room on the left of the bottom deck should probably remain single: there should not be enough space for a bunk bed because it has stairs in its roof area, over the bed. But this fact has to be investigated better; this could also be a twin room, actually, perhaps with the upper bed a little shorter.

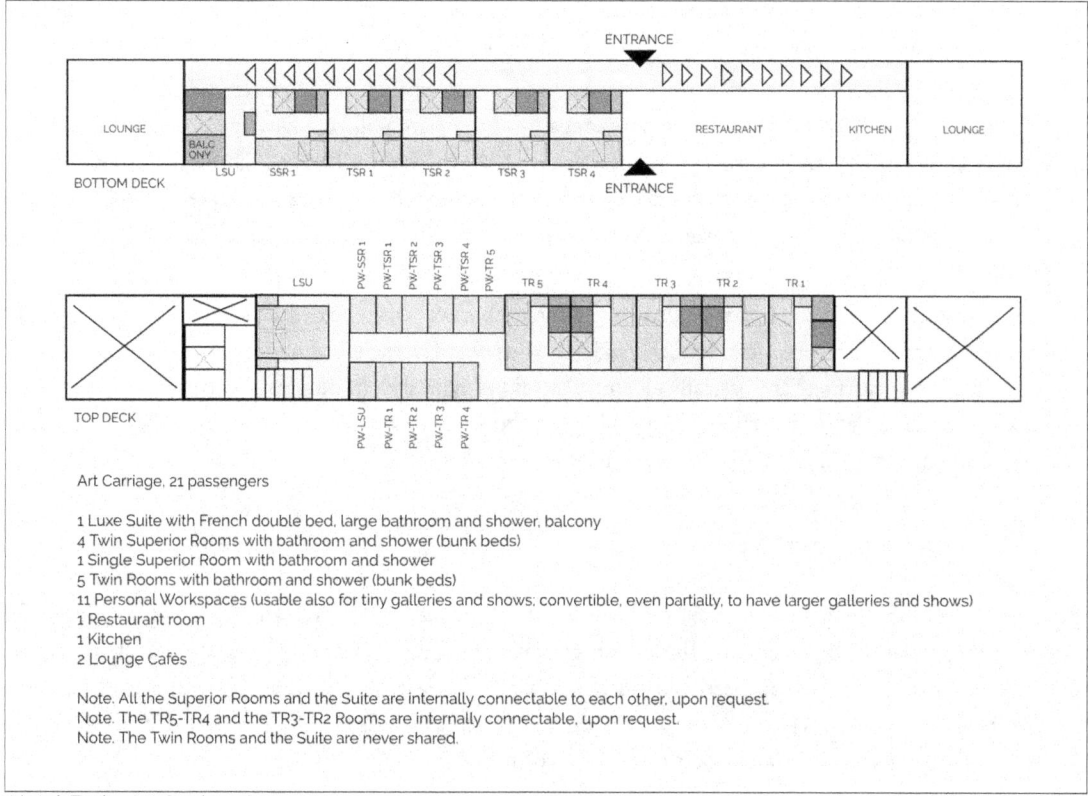

Hotel-Train, Art Carriage layout

Bunk Beds

There is something to say about the bunk beds.

First of all, they are to be avoided in the Business Carriage and Luxe Carriage for obvious reasons (bunk beds do not recall very high standard).

And second, in all the other carriages the bunk beds are acceptable, in my opinion. I say this because:

- if they are well designed and built they are not disreputable, indeed they can be pleasant;
- families and friends often travel together, twin rooms are useful for them;
- twin rooms without bunk beds would take a lot of space, probably too much (because we have also to offer a whole series of other services, in the train);
- the bunk beds must be foldable, to satisfy single-uses of the room; but it is to avoid to use the folding system of the beds during the journey: this is horrible, hospital-like, and would recall standard night trains; so here attendants arrange the beds before guests enter the rooms and the beds always remain in that position;
- even if foldable, beds have to be made with the best quality wood and natural materials for mattress and textiles; and when they are folded, they must disappear completely - not even a hook can appear;
- if a room is booked for single use, the upper bed will disappear; or, at the passenger's choice, the upper bed can stay there and the lower bed can disappear: so that there will be a new space underneath, where attendants can put a table and a chair; practically it would be a workspace inside the room: really wonderful! (...why didn't I think of this before?). A variant, at the passenger's choice, could be to put a sofa - a real sofa, not a bed used like a sofa, and not a train-style couch - in the lower space, obtaining a private lounge: wonderful again!
- the said setting, using the upper bed to have a table/chair or a sofa below, can be replicated also in the Business Carriage, upon request. In fact, I said the Business Carriage has no bunk beds, but in reality it has (because the carriages are basically all-equal, as said previously): in Business Carriage the upper bed is usually always folded inside the wall, invisibly. So, business passengers can have the said setting with upper bed and table/chair or sofa below, if they request it.

The carriages' own styles

Here and in all the carriages, it has to be recalled that it is advisable to have a different internal style for each carriage, to reflect the needs and the characteristics of the probable type of passengers of that carriage. For example, Art Carriage will need art touches, Family Carriage will need simple and safe things as a defence from babies' curiosity, and so on. So, "different carriage, different style", as said in the previous "One hotel, many styles" idea; and prices can vary accordingly.

Service Space of the Art Carriage

In the said Service Space of the Art Carriage there are the same Personal Workspaces we found in the Business Carriage. There is to add here that the Personal Workspaces of the Art Carriage can be used in different ways:

- as a personal laboratory/studio to produce one's own art;
- as a personal art gallery to show and/or sell one's own art;
- as a personal art theatre to show one's own art performances (paid or free);
- as a large art gallery, or a large art theatre, collecting more Workspaces together in some occasions, upon request.

When there are art galleries or art theatres active, properly communicated to all the passengers of the train, other passengers can come to the Art Carriage to visit these galleries or theatres; this could be an interesting activity during the trip.

Idea 6.3
Cinema Carriage

Level 3

The "Cinema Carriage" is exactly like the said Art Carriage, with the only difference that the said Service Space is used here to house a cinema.

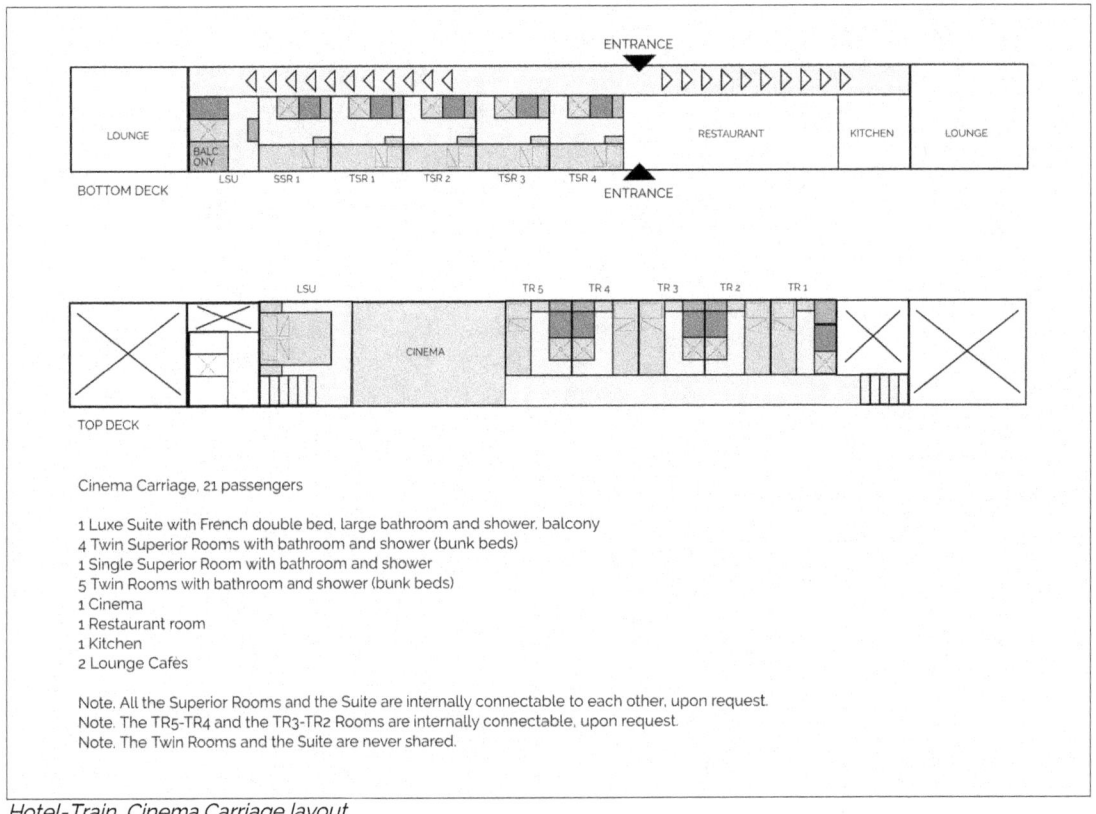

Hotel-Train, Cinema Carriage layout

In the Cinema Carriage (and in the other carriages that will be described below), provided that there aren't external Personal Workspaces available, it could be interesting for single travellers to have their rooms set with bed at the top and workspace with table and chair at the bottom, as said before.

Cinema screen

The screen can be located in the short wall of the cinema room: the left wall in the figure can be used, and an Ultra Short Throw projector could be useful. There should be space for 4 spectators per row, 5 rows, including a 40 cm wide corridor; so the room (around 2,8 x 4,2 m in this figure) could accomodate 20 spectators.

Alternatively, we can have the screen cinema in the long wall of the cinema room, at the top in figure; 7 spectators per row, 3 rows. We'd have a total of 21 spectators.

The seats will not be, in both the cases, as wide armchairs... everything has to be experimented and investigated better.

Cinema and Staff

As in the case of restaurant, the cinema itself is a completely separated space and will have a proper convertible area which will transform in bedroom after the closing time and will disappear within the opening time. It is not necessary to have a dedicated bathroom inside the cinema, because at the bottom deck there is the bathroom of the restaurant (not shown in figure) which is available for both guests and staff.

Idea 6.4
Academy Carriage

Level 3

The "Academy Carriage" layout is identical to the layout of the said Cinema Carriage. Here the said Service Space is used to house an academic room, where someone teaches and other passengers learn, as said previously.

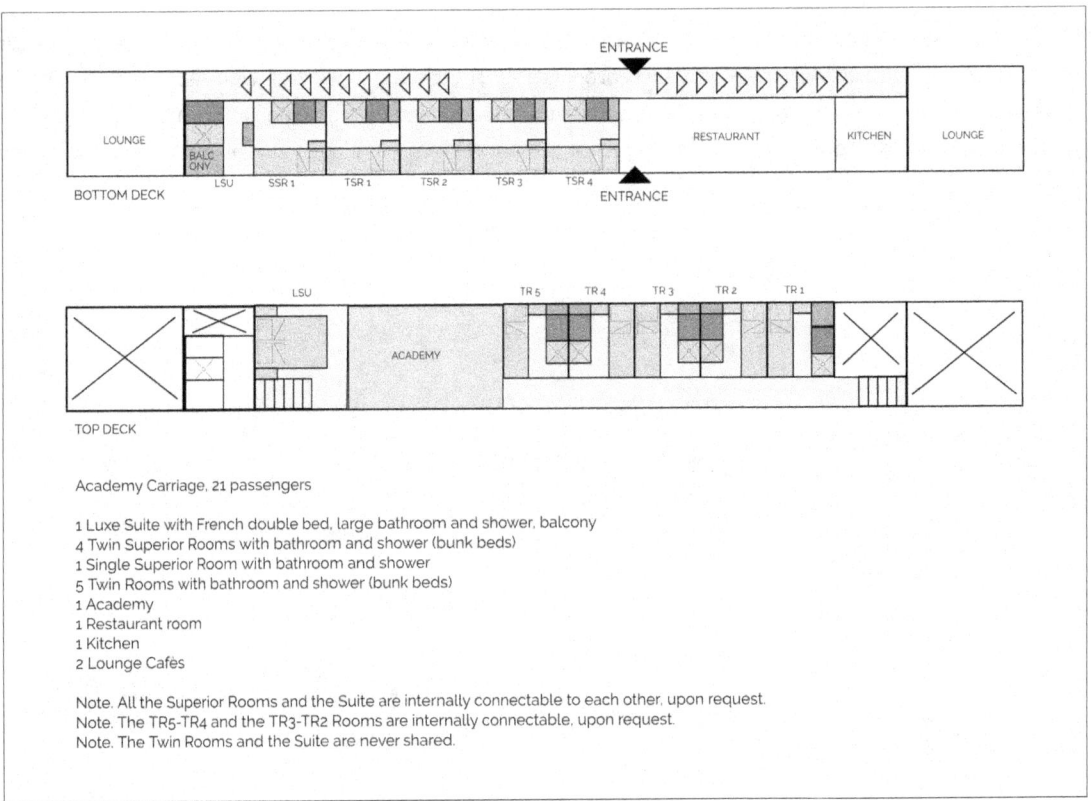

Hotel-Train, Academy Carriage layout

Academy and Teacher

If a teacher is scheduled on a certain trip, it means that the academy room is used for the course taught by that teacher; there are two possibilities here:

- restricted access, for exampe if that course is organised by a school for its students during a school journey;

- non-restricted access, for example if a teacher organises a paid course of a certain subject dedicated to train passengers.

If no teacher is scheduled, the academy room can be used by students and other passengers as it were a study room of the off board libraries, schools and universities.

Academy and Staff

The situation for the academy staff is the same as we have seen previously for the cinema.

Part II - The train   Chapter 6 - Layout design

Idea 6.5
Sport Carriage

Level 3

The "Sport Carriage" is exactly like the said Academy Carriage, with the only difference that the said Service Space is used here to house a gym for fitness exercises, plus a separate playground to practice "tiny ball games".

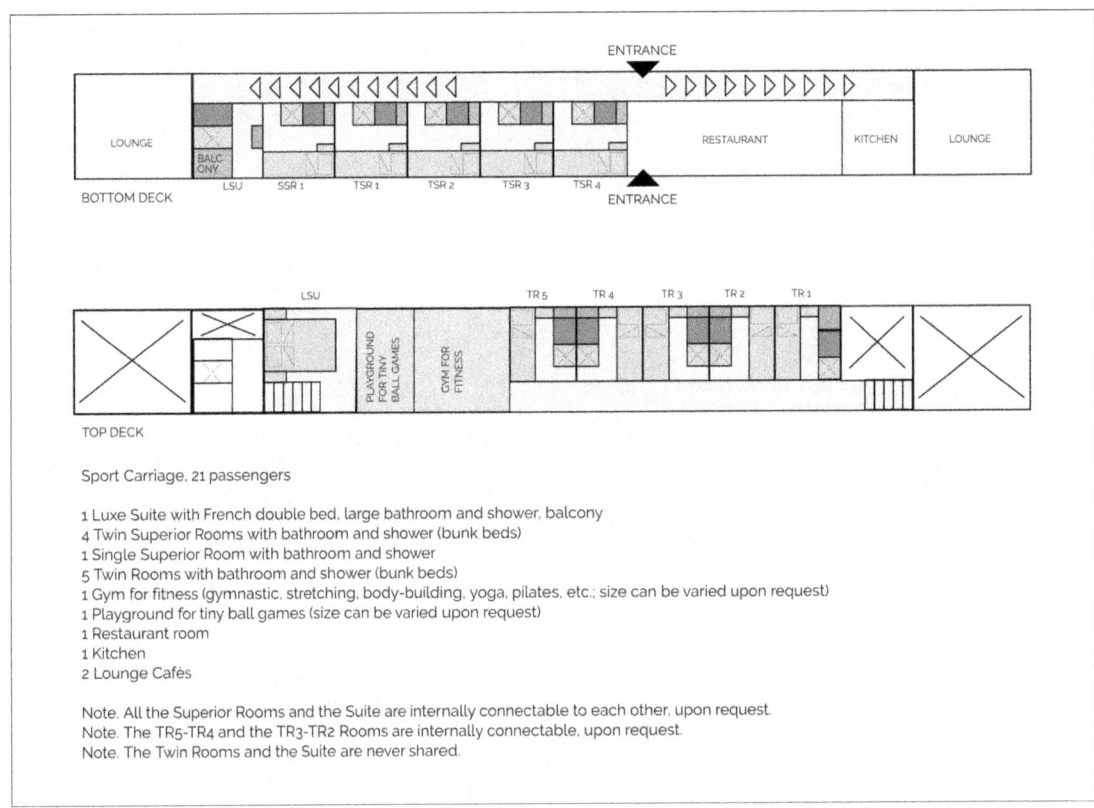

Hotel-Train, Sport Carriage layout

"Tiny ball games"

Some explanation is needed, here. Obviously I'm not thinking about real ball games, they would need... a whole carriage (that is not impossible to think, in reality... it should be investigated). But I experienced that playing with tiny balls, even if in tiny spaces, can be a lot of fun; and, even if you don't run, you move physically when you play with the small ball in a small space. So, let's stop with the constant sitting journeys, and come to the Sport Carriage to play the new sports discipline, Tiny-Basketball!

(...obviously if you prefer there will be also Tiny-Football, Tiny-Volleyball, Tiny-TableTennis, Tiny-Tennis, Tiny-Squash, Tiny-Padel, and so on...)

Gym and Staff

No problem here, gym and playground should not need a stable staff. Should it be necessary, what has already been said for the cinema would apply.

Part II - The train   Chapter 6 - Layout design

Idea 6.6
Shopping Carriage

Level 3

The "Shopping Carriage" layout is identical to the layout of the said Sport Carriage. Here the said Service Space is used to house a shopping center, plus a separate showroom for innovative products.

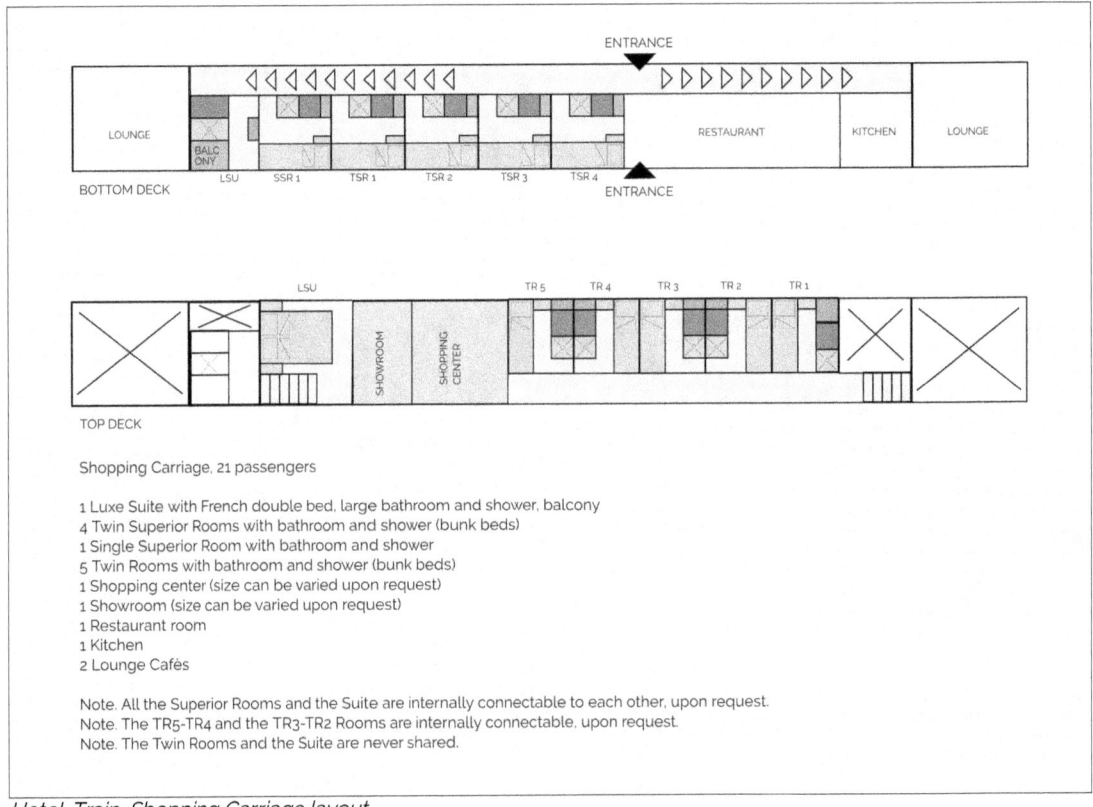

Hotel-Train, Shopping Carriage layout

Shopping Center and Staff

The situation for the shopping/showroom center staff is the same as we have seen previously for the cinema.

Idea 6.7
Touring Carriage

Level 3

The "Touring Carriage" is exactly like the said Shopping Carriage, with the only difference that the said Service Space is used here to house a shop for touring-related items, plus a separate showroom for touring spots, plus an office for tourist informations.

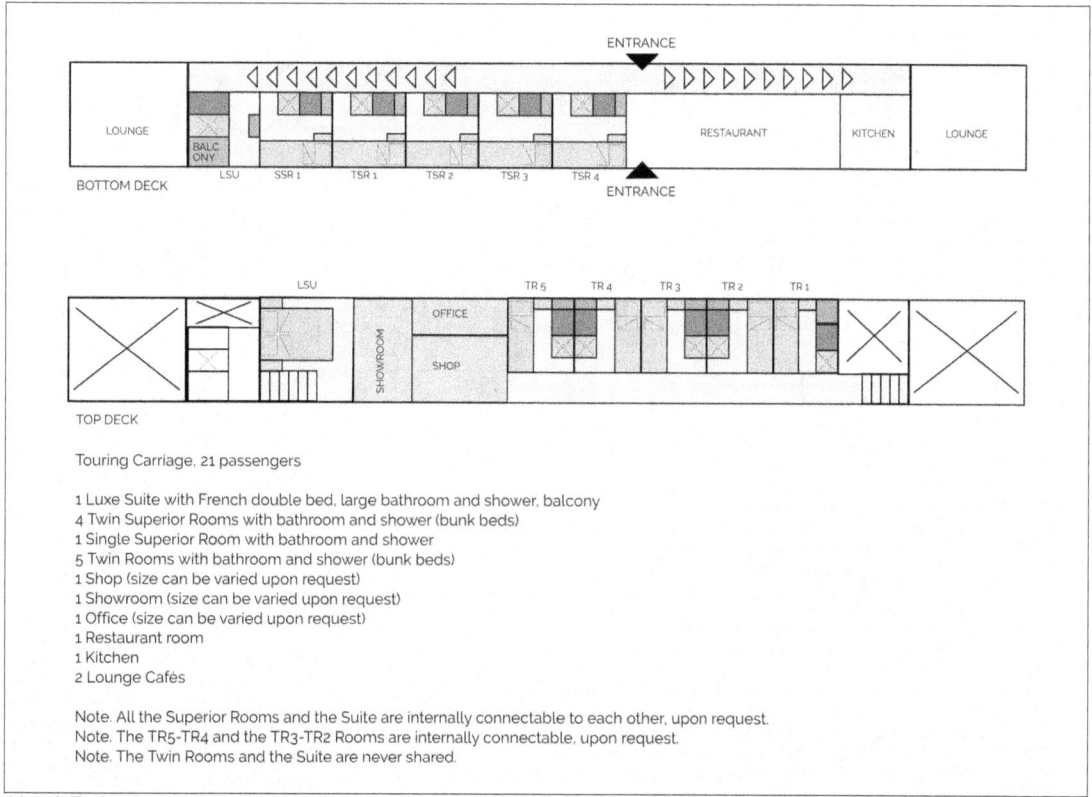

Hotel-Train, Touring Carriage layout

Touring Center and Staff

The situation for the tourist office/shop/showroom staff is the same as we have seen previously for the cinema.

Idea 6.8
Family Carriage

Level 3

The "Family Carriage" layout is identical to the layout of the said Cinema Carriage. Here the said Service Space is used as a playground, where babies and children can play. I think they will have a lot of fun there!

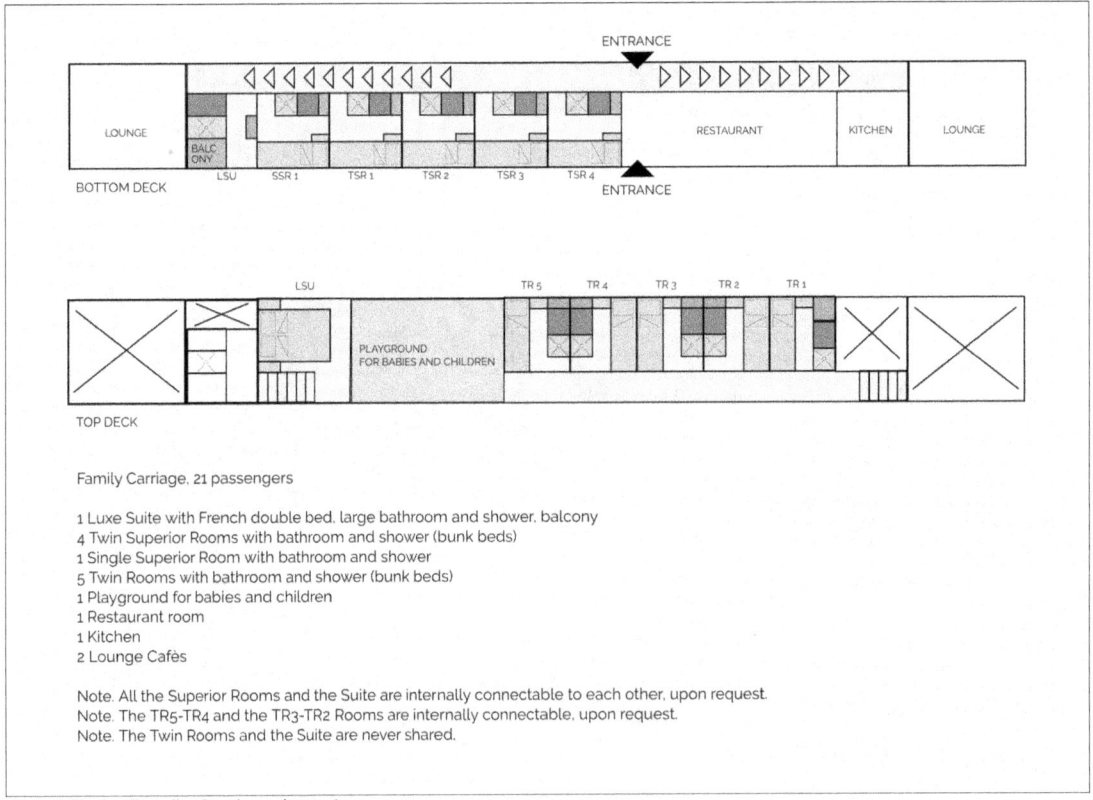

Hotel-Train, Family Carriage layout

Playground and Staff

No problem here, playground should not need a stable staff. Parents are responsible of their children.

Idea 6.9
Bicycle Carriage

Level 3

The "Bicycle Carriage" is like the said Family Carriage, but this time there is an important difference: the space on the lower deck which was used for the restaurant here is used as a parking for bicycles; and the restaurant is moved to the upper deck, in what was called Service Space.

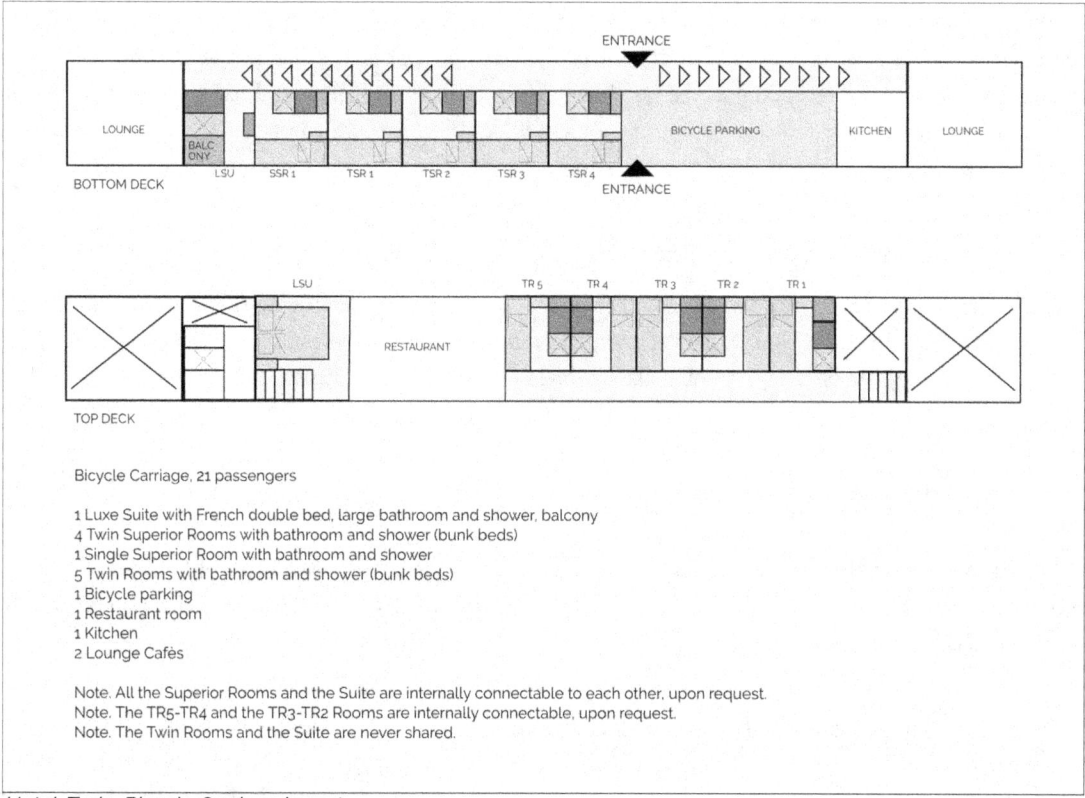

Hotel-Train, Bicycle Carriage layout

"...hey! This way you haven't all-equal carriages, you moved the dining-room upstairs!"

Yes but the structural differences are minimal or even non-existent... I hope it could be possible to manage them. Even the bathroom (not shown in figure) that was of the restaurant can stay exactly where it was, at the bottom deck; it will not be too far from the new upper restaurant. Otherwise the only solution for the bicycle parking would be a separate carriage, like the Cargo Carriage that will be introduced later. But primarily I'd prefer a solution with the bicycle parking inside the passengers' carriage, so that passengers could easily return to their bicycle. In fact, bicycle travellers have always something to do around their bicycle while travelling... bicycles are their pets. Once I saw a traveller who completely disassembled, adjusted and reassembled his bike, inside the running train!

Entrance of bicycles

There is also to say something about the entrance of bicycles. Where do they enter the train? Not through the said main entrance of the Hotel-Train, because with this way the bicycles should ride several carriages before arriving at the parking, with possible discomfort of passengers. So, the bicycles will use the entrances of the Bicycle Carriage...

"...hey! This way you have to take that entrance open! You said one hotel, one entrance!"

Well, yes and no. In reality the door of the Bicycle Carriage can remain always locked usually; it will only be open at the request of the bicycle travellers who need to embark or disembark. Simply the bicycle travellers will go to the reception, at the hotel hall (we'll see it in the following Luxe Carriage), informing about their passage with bicycles; so an attendant will come with them to open the door of the Bicycle Carriage and will stay there to check the open door. After the passage of bicycles, that door will be closed again...

"...hey! This way you waste time! The train has to wait for all these passages of bicycles, to leave!"

Yes, the train must wait, but this is not a problem at all: in fact, remembering the Low Speed idea, the train is scheduled to travel slowly, slower than the characteristics of the railway would allow. So, if the train waits and departs on delay, it will make up for lost time by going a little faster, arriving at the end on time.

Special luggages

There is to add that the Bicycle Carriage is useful also for the previously said "special luggages": they can find a proper space in the bicycle parking. The loading and unloading system of special luggages will be similar to that of bicycles.

Not enough space in the parking area

If, on some occasions, the demand for bicycle and/or special luggages transport is so high that there is not enough space in the parking of the Bicycle Carriage, the surplus bicycles and luggage are placed in the Cargo Carriage which we'll see better in a following paragraph. If more space is required on a certain journey, so that even the Cargo Carriage is not enough, some (possibly rented) ordinary baggage cars can be added to the train composition on demand. Passengers will never be told "there is no room for your bicycle on this train" - as instead ordinary railway companies always say.

Parking and Staff

No problem here, parking should not need a stable staff. Passengers are responsible of their bicycles and special luggages.

Idea 6.10
Luxe Carriage

Level 3

The "Luxe Carriage" is a specialty: quite different from all the other carriages, it retains some elements of the said base layout and changes others.

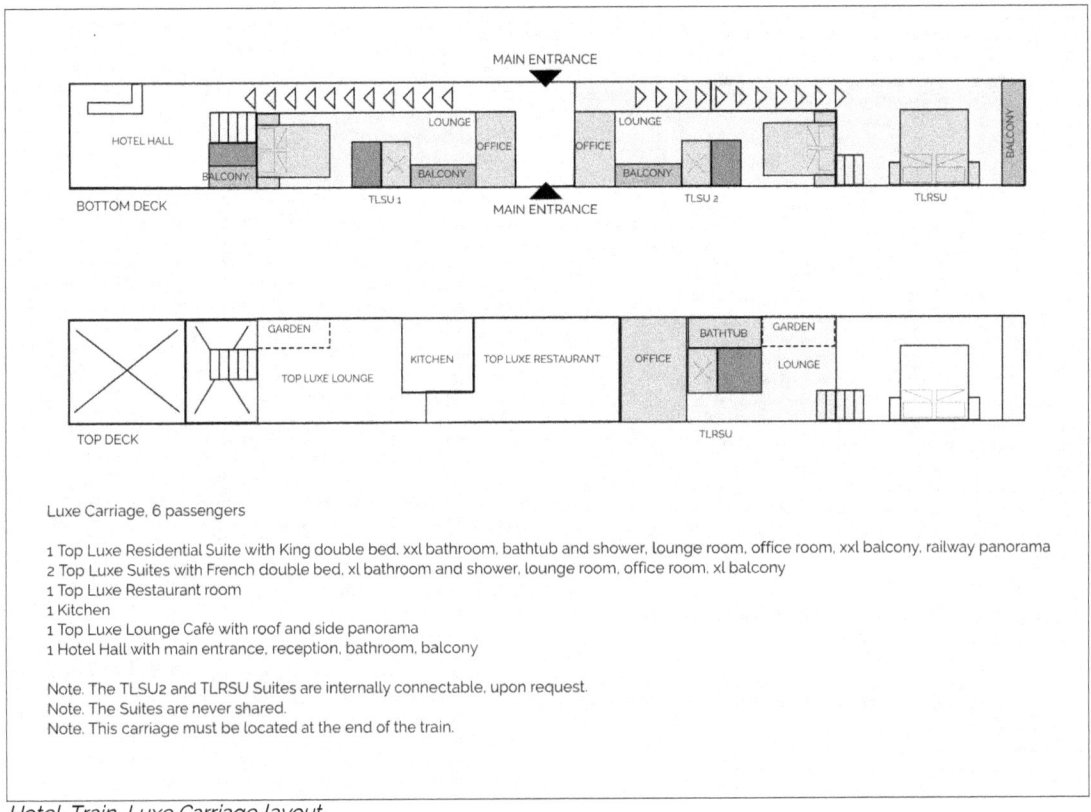

Hotel-Train, Luxe Carriage layout

In this figure, at the "Top Luxe Residential Suite" on the right, you can see where the cover photo of this book came from: exactly from this layout...

"...hey! But that cover photo is non-existent, it's a scam, it's a photomontage of the worst kind!"

Yes, it's a photomontage, but it reflects what the Top Luxe Residential Suite of the train will be: in fact, the layout you see above here will produce almost exactly that photo, when it will be realized in our brand-new, running, Hotel-Train.

"...hey! This way you have a luxury train like the Orient-Express and others! We said we wanted a business train!"

Hotel-Train, Top Luxe Residential Suite - visualsofdana, Kari Shea, Flavio Bassi

Well, no, what I'm designing is not a complete luxury train like the others that exist today; the others are used only for railway cruises and have only luxury carriages in their composition. Here we have only one luxury carriage in the composition of the train, and the other carriages of the train are business, family, etc. The other carriages offer also one of the said cheap-luxe-type suites at higher price; but they remain business, family etc.

Hotel Main Entrance

In the Luxe Carriage there is the main entrance of the hotel, introduced in the previously said "One hotel, one entrance" idea. It is located at the lowest level, to have no stairs arriving from the station platform; from this entrance, you can go with an inclined passage to the hall and reception area (which is a little upper, around 90 cm, because it is over the wheels of the carriage). The hall provides a bathroom and a balcony.

Top Luxe Lounge and Restaurant

From the hall you can go upstairs to the top luxe lounge cafè, which is very panoramic because its roof and side walls are made mostly with glass. You can admire the landscapes, the sky, the stars while sitting on a sofa. There is a garden in the lounge: it will provide beautiful views of flowers and plants, and will hide the inclined passage below (as said describing the entrances and inclined passages of the Business Carriage). The garden will be at an elevation of approximately 90 cm; beyond the garden there will be a sofa, which also hides the sloping passage underneath, at an elevation of approximately 50 cm. The garden can be open-air, beyond a window, or directly inside the lounge.

If you proceed further you enter the well-known, famous, three-stars "The Fork" restaurant. Artistic world class dishes here, in a discreet and muffled atmosphere. There is to add that roof and walls are wood-made in this dining-room - no glass except ordinary windows; this will be to provide a cozy atmosphere. So the windows will be not large; they will be like little paintings on the walls, with their beautiful, refined, frames.

Top Luxe Suites

If you stay on the bottom deck, on the right of the hall in figure, there is the suites area. There are two "Top Luxe Suites" and one "Top Luxe Residential Suite". Unfortunately it seems necessary to have one suite on the left of the main entrance, and the other suites on the right of the main entrance; so they are a bit separate. I can't find another way to have the main entrance at the lowest level, without stairs along the corridor. I'm sorry!

The Top Luxe Suites provide a sleeping area with French double bed, an xl spa bathroom with shower, a lounge room, an office room, an xl balcony. Obviously they feature also all the luxury amenities we can imagine.

The Top Luxe Residential Suite is the top-of-the-top-luxe the train can offer. After its entrance, continuing along the corridor (which is private to the suite, in this part), you arrive in the sleeping area: it features a King double bed, a panoramic all-width window towards the railway, an xxl balcony with space for two chairs and a table. Then, if you go upstairs along its own staircase (large, soft and comfortable, as always), you enter the lounge area, which is panoramic of the sleeping area below and has a garden, similar to the previously said garden of the Top Luxe Lounge. At the upper floor there is also an xxl bathroom with shower and bathtub plus an office room.

"...hey! But all this is completely different from the base model of the Business Carriage! We said we wanted all-equal carriages!"

Yes, this is a special carriage. Basically, it's the only carriage on the train which differs from the others. But I'd say this luxe carriage would be an important investment: these top-luxe lounge, restaurant and suites will provide a very unique vision of the train, with their so large and special spaces, unusual for train environments. And the Residential Suite, with its all-width window on railways, will be the frontman, the cover photo, which will mark our new train in the memory.

Idea 6.11

Cargo Carriage

Level 3

As we said before, there is sometimes a need to transport surplus bicycles or special luggage. There is also to transport all the tools and materials used by the hotel on a daily basis and in special cases. Now, there is probably not enough room for all these things in the passenger carriages: the "Cargo Carriage" is the solution.

Hotel-Train, Cargo Carriage will look like this - James St. John

We need a Cargo Carriage that is linked to the other carriages of the train, to be walkable by both staff and passengers. For this reason, the Cargo Carriage can't be a standard freight carriage; it will be similar to the "baggage car" type; or, even better, to the "combine car" type. Both of these carriage types have existed for a long time but are little used today. The baggage car is dedicated only to carry luggage and bicycles; the combine car is a mixed type with two internal sections: one for luggage/bicycles, and the other for passenger uses (for example a lounge and/or a bathroom). Now, I think we don't need lounges or bathrooms in this Cargo Carriage; but we need another special passenger space... which we'll see better here in the following.

Post Office

Here: if we remember, our Hotel-Train will offer also several types of unusual luggage services (see the "Off-board services" chapter); those services concern shipments and deliveries of luggage made directly *inside* the train, for the maximum comfort of passengers. Good: this Cargo Carriage will be exactly the right place to accommodate a new kind of Post Office, dedicated to those services. Passengers also save a lot of time by using the Cargo Carriage Post Office while travelling, instead of having to go to an external post office before the train departs or after getting off the train upon arrival.

Cargo Carriage finishing

Usual baggage cars were crude and noisy. But we are a Hotel-Train, so our Cargo Carriage will be specially refined to meet the high quality, comfort and accessibility standards of the hotel.

Examples:

Baggage car
https://en.wikipedia.org/wiki/Passenger_railroad_car#Baggage_car

Combine car
https://en.wikipedia.org/wiki/Combine_car

Chapter 7

Experience

Idea 7.1
Available services

Level 3

After the designer period, now is the moment to become a passenger and explore better some aspects of his own experience around our new Hotel-Train. Let's start taking a look at the services which are offered on board.

As said, each carriage offers its own services, in addition to its own restaurant and lounges. And even, all the restaurants and lounges of the train have their own styles and characteristics, related to the corresponding carriages... wonderful! But, who will have access to all these services?

Basically, I'd suggest that any passenger of the train can access any service of the train, top luxe ones included. I'd suggest this because barriers produce always some negative action/reaction somewhere, sometime; and it is better to try to produce positive actions/reactions only, to increase the "aura" of the company.

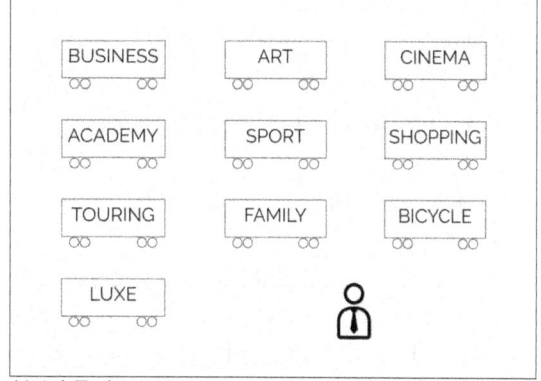

Hotel-Train, any passenger can experience all the services of the train

So the problem of too much crowded spaces could arrive in some case. A solution could be this:

- first of all, all the passengers of a certain carriage (which chose that carriage because they liked the services provided in that carriage) must have a priority access in the services of that carriage; it is to investigate how to provide this priority, it depends on each case;

- second, there will be a reservation system, in which the passengers can reserve a place in any service of the train they would like to experience; these reservations can be made off-board, before the departure of the train, or also on-board, during the train run; it has to be investigated how this reservation system can be reconciled with the said priority access of the carriage-resident passengers;

- third, any service will also be accessible without a reservation, on the fly, if it is not sold out.

Idea 7.2

Paid services and free services

Level 3

There is to consider that there are free services and paid services.

The next services will be free:

- visiting the shopping center and showroom (Shopping Carriage);

- visiting the touring shop, office and showroom (Touring Carriage);

- visiting art galleries (Art Carriage); sometimes, if they involve important pieces of art, they can be paid;

- visiting the balcony of the hall (Luxe Carriage);

- going to the hall and seating (Luxe Carriage);

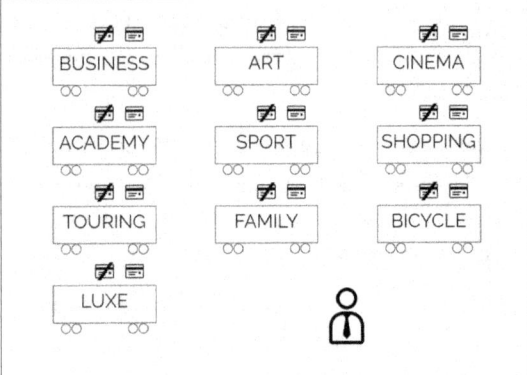

Hotel-Train, each carriage offers free services and paid services

- going to any lounge and seating... "Hey! Why you don't accept only paying guests, in the lounges?" Because we are a Hotel-Train, not a stable-on-the-ground hotel where guests can exit and explore the world; here the train *is* the world, passengers can't go out. So, if we want to change the night train world, it is advisable to offer a lot of interesting places to stay, otherwise the trip is boring... "Hey! I understand, but why you don't offer all these interesting places only to paying guests?" Because interesting places are like air, in our case; you can't ask to pay for air. If you ask to pay for air, some bad action/reaction could create, somewhere, sometime.

And the next services will be paid:

- working and/or having meeting or conference in Personal Workspaces (Business Carriage);

- working and/or showing and/or selling art in Personal Workspaces (Art Carriage);

- attending art shows (Art Carriage);

- going to the cinema (Cinema Carriage);

- going to the academy for a course; or using the academy for one's own use (individual, like a student in a library, or collective, like an entire school lesson); or using the academy to offer a course to passengers (Academy Carriage);

- going to the gym and/or to the playground for tiny ball games (Sport Carriage);
- using the shopping center and/or the showroom for one's own products (Shopping Carriage);
- using the touring shop and/or the touring office and/or the touring showroom for one's own touring spot (Touring Carriage);
- going to the playground for babies and children (Family Carriage);
- storing a bicycle or a special luggage in the parking (Bicycle Carriage);
- getting drinks or snacks at any lounge;
- going to any restaurant to take dinner, breakfast or lunch;
- using the luggage services of the post office (Cargo Carriage).

And what about the previously said reservation system ("Available services" idea)? The paid services usually have it, optionally as said: a passenger may or may not book in advance a certain paid service. And for the free services, it would be advisable to offer them without reservation, for simplicity; however in some case it could be necessary to use the reservation system also for some free service, a finer investigation is needed here.

Idea 7.3
Tickets and services

Level 3

So, what about the tickets? How and when passengers can book a service?

Well, it is simple in reality:

- first of all: when a passenger buy a ticket for a bedroom in a certain carriage, it receives all the services of that carriages included in the price (apart from snacks, drinks amd meals; but they can be included in the ticket as optionals);

- then, if a passenger knows that it would like to experience a service of another carriage, it can reserve a place for that service at the time of ticket purchase; the extra fares will be added to the ticket's price;

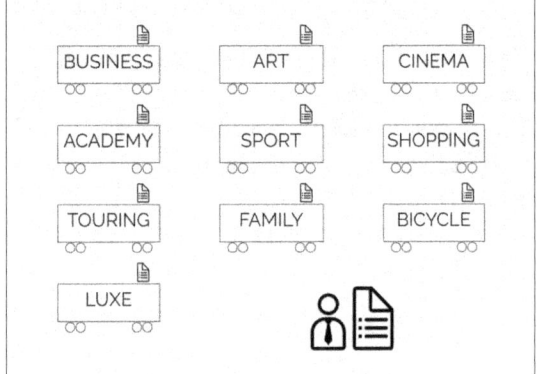

Hotel-Train, all the services can be booked off or on board the train

but, attention here: it can't be guaranteed that the purchased service will be really available, because it could be sold-out due to the corresponding carriage-resident passengers - which have priority as said before; so during the run of the train the status of the reservation could be modified to "unavailable" (and the rejected passenger will be refunded);

- the same reservation system can be used also after the ticket purchase: at any moment before the train departure or also during the train run, as said; the extra fares to pay will be charged in the said Universal Transport Card of the passenger;

- during the train run it is possible to access any service even without reservation, if that service is not sold-out; as mentioned above, just go to the entrance of the service with your Universal Transport Card and enter. Very simple.

Generic Ticket

I go to buy the ticket for my favourite carriage (let's say "Business") and I discover that my type of carriage is 100% full, sold out all over the train. What can I do? I have two ways:

- I can buy a ticket in another type of carriage which still has available places. For example, if I know that my second choice is "Sport", I check the Sport Carriage: oh, there is the last room. Perfect! Booked.

- I can buy a "Generic Ticket". What is the Generic Ticket? It's a ticket which has no speciality added, and can be located in any carriage of the train. For example, if I was looking for a Single Room, I buy a "Single Room Generic Ticket". The system proposes me the carriage which has, at that moment, the lowest occupancy of the train: there are rooms available. Perfect! Booked.

Here there is a note to add: it should be not possible to choose another carriage, in case of Generic Tickets; only the carriage proposed by the system can be booked with a Generic Ticket. This is because, in order to maximise passenger satisfaction, it is better for the most popular carriages to remain available for passengers who will be looking for exactly those types of carriages; in fact, this way minimises the number of passengers who will look for a certain type of carriage and find it sold out.

The Generic Ticket can have lower fares, because it has no speciality added: no Personal Workspace, no Cinema, No Gym, and so on. If I like to add some speciality of a certain type, I can book a reservation for that speciality: for example, for the Cinema. But if the Cinema will have no places available at my moment, because of the Cinema Carriage resident passengers, my reservation - as said before - will be set as "unavailable" and refunded.

No Personal Workspaces available

There is also to note that, for passengers who needed a Personal Workspace (which is offered by the Business and Art Carriages) and find that all the Business and Art Carriages are sold out, a good solution exists: buy any ticket (the Generic Ticket is also fine) for a Twin Room with Single Use, and choose to use the upper bed with the table/chair set below (as said in the presentation of bunk beds, "Art Carriage" idea). This way they will have their work space in the room. Also all suites offer space for a table/chair set, but they are more expensive.

Idea 7.4
The Gift

Level 3

This, I know, is another mad idea of mine. And yet it seems so important to me... It appeared this morning, while I was admiring my work about the carriages layout. I looked at all those beautiful and various corridors, lounges, cafès... art rooms, cinemas, offices... all that inside a train! I was getting into the heart of a passenger, while he was walking along the carriages, astonished by the vision of such impossible spaces. And I felt the heart of that passenger broken, when he arrived in front of the door of the Top Luxe Suites area in the Luxe Carriage: closed passage, locked, a barrier behind which a paradise-for-train-enthusiasts is hidden... a paradise that the passenger - he knows - will never taste, because the price of the Top Luxe Suites is not affordable for him, and it will never be affordable...

So I thought: no, we can't do that, there is something wrong here. We cannot break anyone's heart! We must make all our passengers happy.

There must be a solution... cancel the top luxe, maybe? But why... it is so astonishing... it would be a pity...

And a possible solution appeared: "The Gift".

It's a simple system: when the train will be not sold-out, some time before the departure of the train all available rooms and suites will be offered to some passengers who purchased lower fare tickets. No extra charge asked, not even symbolic: the free rooms will be given as a gift. How to choose the passengers which will receive The Gift? I don't know exactly at this moment but... maybe one possibility could be to choose at random; or maybe early-bird passengers, who purchased the ticket with more advance than others, and/or frequent travellers, who travel with us often, could be privileged (to reward their interest).

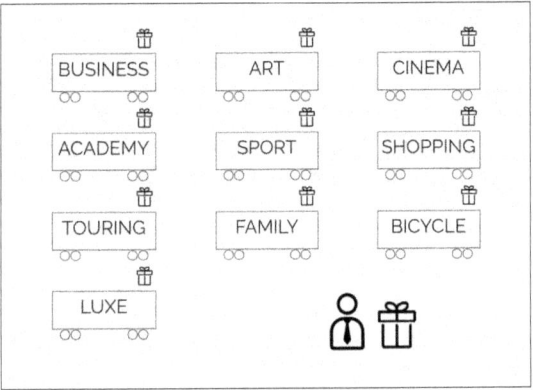

Hotel-Train, The Gift avoids possible disappointment in passengers

I have to say that a similar system is already existing in air companies. But they never will give an Etihad "The Residence" comparable place to a passenger who purchased an Economy class ticket. Instead our new The Gift system will do. Even the Top Luxe Residential Suite can be a gift, if not sold-out.

There is to add that the more expensive accomodations will be offered as a gift, but the passengers could also refuse them because for some reason they could like to stay in a certain room of a certain carriage.

In addition, The Gift will contain also the usual mileage point reward system, already used in air and railway companies. This will offer journeys in the Top Luxe Suites among the various awards.

Overall, The Gift seems a simple system to transform the broken heart in a hoping heart. Sadness will no longer form in front of that locked door, because there will always be hope of being able to experience that incredible residential train accomodation. Positive actions/reactions should appear.

Idea 7.5
Delayed passengers

Level 3

What happens if some passengers are late arriving at the station for their train departure? Does the train leave without them?

No, this happens in ordinary trains and night trains, not here. As said previously, our Hotel-Train has no hurry: remembering the said Low Speed concept, the train is scheduled to travel slowly, slower than the characteristics of the railway would allow. So, if the train waits and departs on delay, it will make up for lost time by going a little faster, arriving at the end on time.

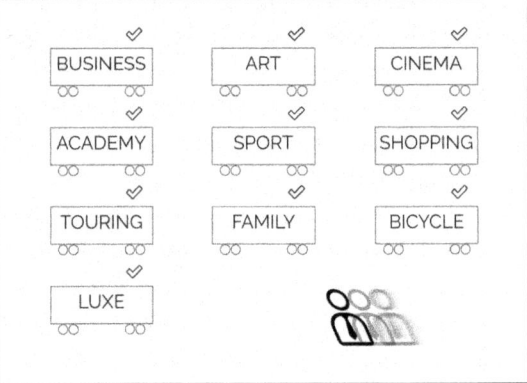

Hotel-Train, the train waits for delayed passengers

This means that the train can wait for the delays of passengers: they should call or contact the company to inform about their delay. If they do not inform, the company tries to contact the delayed passengers. If a contact is impossible, the train waits for a maximum amount of time (30 minutes or one hour, for example); then at the end, if there are no news, leaves. If the delay will mean higher fares to pay for the use of the station, something can be charged to passengers... investigation needed.

Idea 7.6
Room comparison

Level 3

In the next table we see the main characteristics of the different rooms, at a glance.

HOTEL-TRAIN ROOMS	BED	BED SPACE	BATHROOM	SHOWER	BATHTUBE	OFFICE	LOUNGE	BALCONY
LUXE CARRIAGE TOP LUXE RESIDENTIAL	1x DOUBLE (KING)	XXL	1x (XXL)	1x (XXL)	1x (XXL)	1x (XXL)	1x (XXL)	1x (XXL)
LUXE CARRIAGE TOP LUXE	1x DOUBLE (FRENCH)	XL	1x (XL)	1x (XL)	-	1x (XL)	1x (XL)	1x (XL)
BUSINESS CARRIAGE LUXE	1x DOUBLE (FRENCH)	L	1x (L)	1x (L)	-	-	-	1x (L)
BUSINESS CARRIAGE SINGLE SUPERIOR	1x SINGLE	M	1x (M)	1x (M)	-	-	-	-
BUSINESS CARRIAGE SINGLE	1x SINGLE	S	1x (M)	1x (M)	-	-	-	-
OTHER CARRIAGES LUXE	1x DOUBLE (FRENCH)	L	1x (L)	1x (L)	-	-	-	1x (L)
OTHER CARRIAGES SINGLE SUPERIOR	1x SINGLE	M	1x (M)	1x (M)	-	-	-	-
OTHER CARRIAGES TWIN SUPERIOR	2x SINGLE (BUNK)	M	1x (M)	1x (M)	-	-	-	-
OTHER CARRIAGES TWIN	2x SINGLE (BUNK)	S	1x (M)	1x (M)	-	-	-	-

Idea 7.7
Carriage comparison

Level 3

In the next table we see the main characteristics of the different carriages, at a glance.

HOTEL-TRAIN CARRIAGES (BEDS)	SUITES	ROOMS	RESTAURANT	LOUNGE CAFÈ	SPECIALITY	HALL	BATHROOM	BALCONY
LUXE (6)	1x TOP LUXE RESID 2x TOP LUXE	-	1x (luxe)	1x (luxe)	2x PANORAMA (lounge, balcony)	1x	1x (hall)	1x
BUSINESS (12)	1x LUXE	5x SINGLE SUP 5x SINGLE	1x	2x	12x WORKSPACES	-	1x (restaurant)	-
ART (21)	1x LUXE	1x SINGLE SUP 4x TWIN SUP 5x TWIN	1x	2x	12x WORKSPACES	-	1x (restaurant)	-
CINEMA (21)	1x LUXE	1x SINGLE SUP 4x TWIN SUP 5x TWIN	1x	2x	1x CINEMA	-	1x (restaurant)	-
ACADEMY (21)	1x LUXE	1x SINGLE SUP 4x TWIN SUP 5x TWIN	1x	2x	1x ACADEMY	-	1x (restaurant)	-
SPORT (21)	1x LUXE	1x SINGLE SUP 4x TWIN SUP 5x TWIN	1x	2x	1x GYM 1x PLAYGROUND	-	1x (restaurant)	-
SHOPPING (21)	1x LUXE	1x SINGLE SUP 4x TWIN SUP 5x TWIN	1x	2x	1x SHOP 1x SHOWROOM	-	1x (restaurant)	-
TOURING (21)	1x LUXE	1x SINGLE SUP 4x TWIN SUP 5x TWIN	1x	2x	1x TOURIST OFFICE 1x SHOP 1x SHOWROOM	-	1x (restaurant)	-
FAMILY (21)	1x LUXE	1x SINGLE SUP 4x TWIN SUP 5x TWIN	1x	2x	1x PLAYGROUND	-	1x (restaurant)	-
BICYCLE (21)	1x LUXE	1x SINGLE SUP 4x TWIN SUP 5x TWIN	1x (top deck)	2x	1x PARKING (bottom deck)	-	1x (parking)	-
CARGO (0)	-	-	-	-	1x CARGO 1x POST OFFICE	-	-	-

Idea 7.8
Complete rolling train

Level 3

Here we see what the new train will be, with its complete rolling team of carriages. As previously said, the train composition will vary depending on the demands of the different types of passengers, which will vary in different seasons. Here we see an example of compositions in different seasons.

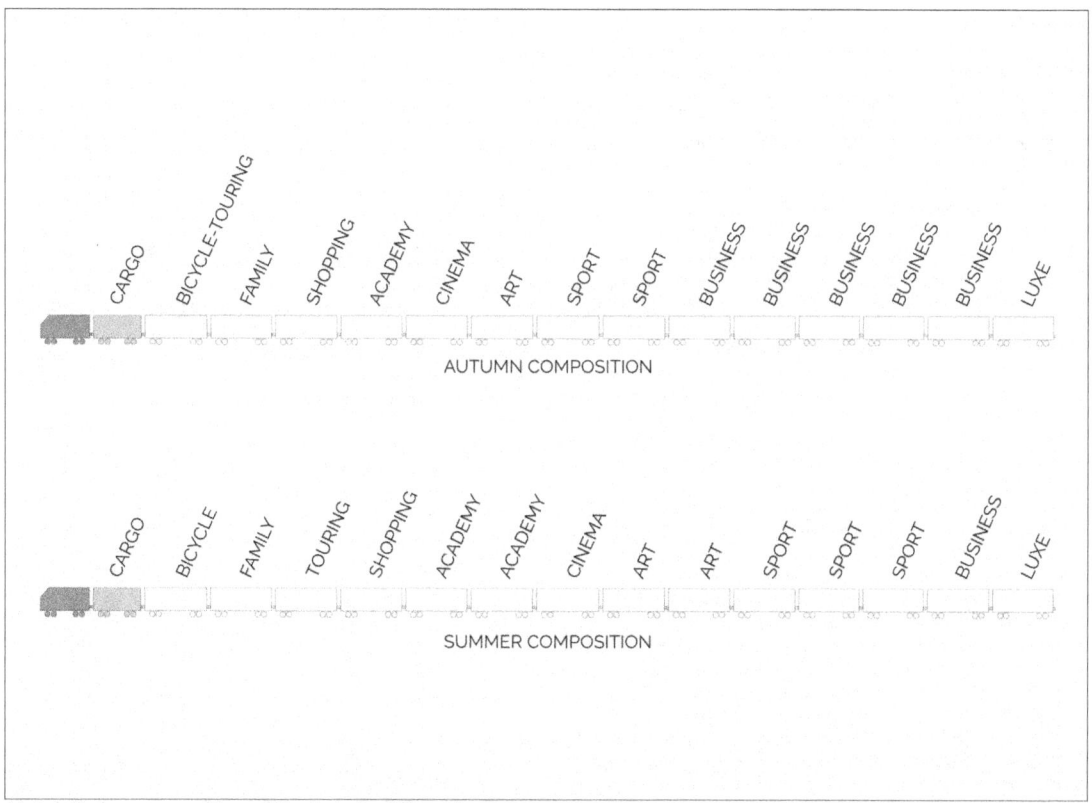

Hotel-Train, composition of the train in different seasons

As said, the Luxe Carriage has to be at the end of the train, because of the panoramic window of its Top Luxe Residential Suite. The Business, which are the second most expensive carriages, are placed close to the Luxe. Then we have the Sport Carriages, which can be often used by the Business and Luxe passengers (they paid the highest fares, so the services most useful for them are placed close to them). Then the Art and Cinema Carriages, which also can be used by Business and Luxe passengers. Then the Academy, close to Cinema and Art because there could be links between them. Then the Shopping and Touring Carriages, useful for all the passengers of the train. Then the most "isolated" areas (I mean, they should not be of interest to the non-resident passengers): Family and Bicycle Carriages.

At the beginning of the train there is the Cargo Carriage, which is used to store the surplus bicycles and special luggages, as well as the tools and materials used in the train. The Cargo Carriage, located at the beginning of the train, also has the advantage of protecting all passengers from the locomotive, which always produces noise and stressing electromagnetic fields. The aim here should be to have the Cargo Carriage in addition to the ordinary number of passenger carriages of the train; i.e. if the train has 14 passenger carriages, the Cargo Carriage should be the 15th. It should not be a problem to go with the Cargo Carriage beyond the normal station platforms, in case they are not long enough. But further investigation is needed here.

The Cargo Carriage also houses the said Post Office; passengers can come here to send or receive their luggage while travelling, as said introducing the unusual luggage services (see the "Off-board services" chapter).

If, in some season, the demand of some type of passengers is so low that it does not fill a carriage, it can be used a mixed carriage as shown in the example figure.

Chapter 8

Business plan

Idea 8.1
Expected fares

Level 3

After the passenger period, now is the time to become a manager. Let's start trying to calculate the different fares we can expect to offer, for a certain route between the A town and the B town.

First of all I have to say that in my design the new Hotel-Train will run all year long, all the days. This because it is not only a business train (which will not run during holidays) but it has several types of carriages, dedicated to different types of passengers as said before; and in addition it is easy to change the composition of the train in the different seasons, depending on the demand of each type of passenger in each season, because the carriages are almost completely all-equal: it needs only to use the said Modularity idea and work to provide a proper setting of the said Service Space and of the carriage style in the different seasons, to obtain the right train composition valid for each season. It is possible to change the train composition even in the single working days and holidays within a single week. So the whole train should have passengers in all the days of the year.

EXPECTED FARES SIMULATION - PRICES IN EUR	PER ROOM	PER PERSON
LUXE CARRIAGE TOP LUXE RESIDENTIAL SUITE	1940	970
LUXE CARRIAGE TOP LUXE SUITE	970	485
BUSINESS CARRIAGE LUXE SUITE	780	390
BUSINESS CARRIAGE SINGLE SUPERIOR ROOM	350	350
BUSINESS CARRIAGE SINGLE ROOM	270	270
OTHER CARRIAGES LUXE SUITE	780	390
OTHER CARRIAGES SINGLE SUPERIOR ROOM	350	350
OTHER CARRIAGES TWIN SUPERIOR ROOM	350	175
OTHER CARRIAGES TWIN ROOM	270	135

Hotel-Train, expected fares

Let's take the simplest case, separated AB and BA routes. We need two trains: in each day one goes from A to B and the other from B to A. In this route let's say that, for the whole year, the total cost for the company is X and that the company wants a gain of Y. So the passengers must spend, in the whole year, the following:

total amount spent by passengers yearly = Z = X + Y

That amount of Z has to come from the ticket fares (let's forget by now the extra services like restaurants etc., for simplicity).

Now. In any day we have two running trains, let's say with 14 carriages each. So we have a total of 28 running carriages. It follows that each carriage, on any day, must have a total income from tickets like the following:

expected income of each carriage daily = K = Z / 365 / 28

That K amount has to be shared between the different rooms of each carriage, depending on the level of each room. We have to build a schema of coefficients similar to this:

- Luxe: Top Luxe Residential = 50%
- Luxe: Top Luxe = 25%

- Business: Luxe = 20%
- Business: Single Superior = 9%
- Business: Single = 7%

- Others: Luxe = 20%
- Others: Single Superior = 9%
- Others: Twin Superior = 9%
- Others: Twin = 7%

Now, I read somewhere an example in which for a certain European route of a night train it was expected (in that example, I don't know if it is realistic or not) the following total cost for the two running trains:

total cost for two running trains yearly = X = 30 million eur

Let's say that the company plans a gross gain of 20% of the total cost:

total gross gain for two running trains yearly = $Y = X * 0,20$ = 6 million eur

So we have:

total amount spent by passengers yearly = $Z = X + Y$ = 36 million eur

expected income of each carriage daily = $K = Z / 365 / 28$ = 3500 eur approx.

At the end the result of the fares for each one-night journey would be:

- Luxe: Top Luxe Residential = $K * 0,50$ = 1750 eur per room = 875 eur per person
- Luxe: Top Luxe = $K * 0,25$ = 875 eur per room = 437,5 eur per person

- Business: Luxe = $K * 0,20$ = 700 eur per room = 350 eur per person
- Business: Single Superior = $K * 0,09$ = 315 eur per room = 315 eur per person
- Business: Single = $K * 0,07$ = 245 eur per room = 245 eur per person

- Others: Luxe = $K * 0,20$ = 700 eur per room = 350 eur per person
- Others: Single Superior = $K * 0,09$ = 315 eur per room = 315 eur per person

- Others: Twin Superior = K * 0,09 = 315 eur per room = 157,5 eur per person
- Others: Twin = K * 0,07 = 245 eur per room = 122,5 eur per person

However this would be true if the train were 100% full, in all the days. Hopefully it will be. But more realistically (and remaining optimistic) we could imagine an average occupancy coefficient like the following:

average occupancy coefficient = P = 0,90

i.e. the train should be 90% full, on average. The final, corrected fares will be the following:

- Luxe: Top Luxe Residential = K * 0,50 / P = 1944 eur per room = 972 eur per person
- Luxe: Top Luxe = K * 0,25 / P = 972 eur per room = 486 eur per person

- Business: Luxe = K * 0,20 / P = 777 eur per room = 388,5 eur per person
- Business: Single Superior = K * 0,09 / P = 350 eur per room = 350 eur per person
- Business: Single = K * 0,07 / P = 272 eur per room = 272 eur per person

- Others: Luxe = K * 0,20 / P = 777 eur per room = 388,5 eur per person
- Others: Single Superior = K * 0,09 / P = 350 eur per room = 350 eur per person
- Others: Twin Superior = K * 0,09 / P = 350 eur per room = 175 eur per person
- Others: Twin = K * 0,07 / P = 272 eur per room = 136 eur per person

Oh, this is really astonishing: even the Top Luxe Residential Suite has a human price, it is not priced like the said Etihad "The Residence", which costed around 10000-20000 $ for one trip. These seem really perfect prices for a one-night journey in our new, super comfortable and interesting, Hotel-Train... these prices are also much cheaper than what luxury trains ask for their one-night routes.

There is to add that these are base fares, valid if all the carriages had the same costs for the company. In reality some modification in the fares of the different types of carriage will be possible, depending on the different costs for the company due to the services which will be really offered in each type of carriage. At the end some carriage could increase these base fares a little, and some other could decrease them a little.

Idea 8.2
Comparison with the OBB case

Level 3

We can have a verification of the total cost we considered in the previous example, and of the corresponding fares we obtained, comparing what the excellent OBB does. OBB is the main company of European night trains of today, and as far as I know (could be wrong) it obtains a net gain from the night trains it manages.

COMPARISON WITH OBB SIMULATION - PRICES IN EUR	OBB	HOTEL-TRAIN	HOTEL-TRAIN +40%
TOTAL REVENUE PER CARRIAGE	5000	3500	4900
SINGLE ROOM	240	270	380
TWIN ROOM PER ROOM	380	270	380
TWIN ROOM PER PERSON	190	135	190

Hotel-Train, comparison with OBB

1) Comfortline sleeping cars - 4000 eur

According to what seat61 says, the Comfortline sleeping car is used in almost all the routes, and provides 3 Deluxe compartments and 9 normal compartments. All the compartments can be sold as single, double or triple (1 bed, 2 bunk beds or 3 bunk beds).

Let's try to buy a ticket, for example, for the Innsbruck-Amsterdam route, Sat, 22 Oct 2022. It's Saturday so it is the most expensive, looking at the OBB website. The OBB website confirms that there are normal and Deluxe compartments, but unexpectedly the website does not allow me to choose the Deluxe option; I suppose that all the compartments are offered at the same price, and the first passengers receive the Deluxe (...I don't want to think that Deluxe are... hidden somewhere to... take them secretly available for the best travellers maybe... no, it's impossible, it's Austrian!).

- If I set a 1 bed compartment, the price is 240 eur per person; so the total compartment takes 240 eur in total.
- If I set a 2 beds compartment, the price is 190 eur per person; so the total compartment takes 380 eur in total.
- If I set a 3 beds compartment, the price is 170 eur per person; so the total compartment takes 510 eur in total.

Now, we don't know how many single, double or triple are usually purchased; let's imagine around 1/3 for each, for simplicity. So the total income of the Comfortline carriage 100% full would be:

total income of Comfortline Carriage 100% full = T_{100} = (4 * 510) + (4 * 380) + (4 * 240) = 4520 eur

If we set a 90% occupancy coefficient, we obtain:

total income of Comfortline Carriage 90% full = T_{90} = T_{100}*0,90 = 4068 eur

2) Couchette cars - 5500 eur

According to what seat61 says, the Couchette car provides 9 compartments. All the compartments can be sold as 4 beds or 6 beds

I try to buy the ticket for the same said trip. I obtain the following.

- If I set a 4 beds compartment, the price is 140 eur per person; so the total compartment takes 560 eur in total.
- If I set a 6 beds compartment, the price is 130 eur per person; so the total compartment takes 780 eur in total.

Now, we don't know how many 4 beds or 6 beds are usually purchased; let's imagine around 1/2 for each, for simplicity. So the total income of the Couchette carriage 100% full would be:

total income of Couchette Carriage 100% full = T_{100} = (5 * 780) + (4 * 560) = 6140 eur

If we set a 90% occupancy coefficient, we obtain:

total income of Couchette Carriage 90% full = T_{90} = T_{100}*0,90 = 5526 eur

3) Seating cars - 6000 eur

According to what seat61 says, the Seating car provides 6-seater compartments. Seat61 doesn't say how many compartments are in the carriage; let's imagine 10 compartments.

I try to buy the ticket for the same said trip. I obtain the following.

- The price is 110 eur per person; so the total compartment takes 660 eur in total.

So the total income of the Seating carriage 100% full would be:

total income of Seating Carriage 100% full = T_{100} = (10 * 660) = 6600 eur

If we set a 90% occupancy coefficient, we obtain:

total income of Seating Carriage 90% full = T_{90} = T_{100}*0,90 = 5940 eur

There is to consider that I took the base, higher fares (the flexible ones); there will be discounts for non-refundable fares. For example a place in the OBB seating carriage would cost 30 eur only (!) at this moment, Sun, August 14 2022, with the non-refundable fare.

Conclusions of the comparison

The conclusions of this comparison are encouraging:

- each OBB night carriage of any type, 90% full, gets around 5000 eur; this is 40% more than what was said in the previous "Expected fares" simulation, where it was found that each carriage should get 3500 eur to cover all the costs and gains. However the two values, 5000 and 3500, are comparable, they are not completely different. So that simulation seems not bad... maybe the resulting expected fares could be increased by that 40%, for example. Fine investigation is needed here.

- the prices of OBB are very similar to what was found in the said "Expected fares" simulation: single bedroom for 240 eur in OBB, 270 eur in the said simulation; bed in double for 190 eur in OBB, 135 in the said simulation. So the prices of the said simulation seem perfectly sellable for a one-night train trip (remember that OBB is an excellent example because it runs night trains with profit). Veeeeery good!

Data from:
https://www.seat61.com/trains-and-routes/nightjet.htm
https://www.nightjet.com/en/

Idea 8.3
Replacement Carriages

Level 3

There is a need for one (or more) replacement carriage to be considered. The replacement carriage is necessary to deal with situations in which some carriages are broken down, need maintenance and cannot travel. With no replacement carriages available, the company cannot offer the services already sold with tickets for a certain journey, resulting in inextricable problems and passenger dissatisfaction.

Hotel-Train, Replacement Carriages

Standard Replacement

> "...hey! How many replacement carriages you need? You have too many carriage types!"

Yes, there are many carriage types, but the management of their replacements is not complicated in reality. In fact, there is to remember that all the carriage types (except the Luxe carriage, which needs a separate speech) come from the same base model, the Business Carriage type. Only the said Service Space varies. So, we can have only one "Standard Replacement Carriage" which will be of that base model, and attendants will set the Service Space accordingly to the needed replacement. The Service Space is a 12 sqm open space, in the previously said layout; it should be not so complicated to set: there will be only to arrange some secundary wall and the furniture.

> "...hey! You said different carriages, different style, so you have to change also the carriage style!"

True, there is also the carriage style to set accordingly to the type that has to be replaced. So there will be also some work to do inside the bedrooms, restaurants and lounges. It will need a quite big staff, to do all this work in a right time. But it is not impossible to have a large staff to set the Standard Replacement Carriage with the right flavour; it should be cheaper than having different models of carriages, each one with its own replacement. And in addition, it is not necessary to repeat the identical usual internal style of the ordinary carriages; for the replacement carriage, a generic style with few personal touches of the type of carriage to be replaced will be fine.

Luxe Replacement

About the Luxe Carriage, it needs a different "Luxe Replacement Carriage" because its layout is very different. So costs increase; but it seems to me that Luxe Carriage should be an important investment, because it provides some special, unique, dream-spaces to offer - while the fares, as said before, should be not so impossible for humans, also for the Top Luxe Residential Suite (at least in some special occasions, like gifts, celebrations, birthdays, etc.). I hope the investment for its replacement could be affordable by the company.

Cargo Replacement

We also have the said Cargo Carriage to consider, because that could also break down. Here, to keep costs down, we could replace it with an ordinary baggage carriage hired for the occasion.

Conclusions

Wow! What a rush... the end of this work seems to have arrived. I don't know exactly how and why but, since my wife went to her family in Japan for a month, taking our little baby on the road, I irresistibly felt the need to write down everything that was in my head, about this new Hotel-Train concept. From the morning to the evening, always. My mind was like a volcano during this month, an unstoppable outpouring of incandescent lava, and every day a new mass of it arrived... I let you imagine how I spent these hot August days - while I was terrified at the thought of getting a phone call with the wife asking "Did you put the house in order?".

I'll tell you a secret (please do not read here if you have not read the whole book first): the imaginary new railway company really exists. I never will say its name! But the fact is that the collaboration was really only imaginary... in the reality I simply contacted the company and proposed some of the first contents of this book. But, provided that it was August, the company was on holiday - so I had to wait until September to see if any interesting replies come in. I actually received a reply, I was afraid to open it and waited a few days, but when I opened it... I saw that it was just an automatic reply, talking about reopening next September. And so my mind began to erupt on its own, and so this book in around a fortnight is here. Life is so fun, sometimes.

I have to thank JekK, Milano Lounge and Glenti FM. They gave me the soundtrack for this month, making me feel good while I was surrounded by all that.

And I thank all Readers, for their interest about this work and for having shared some of their time with me.

I wish you all the best,

Flavio

> Note. Would you like to be involved in the Hotel-Train project? I still don't know if and how, but maybe a group of Hotel-Train enthusiasts could form. In any case, if you like to write me about anything, please use the "Contacts" page of this book.

> Here is JekK - directly from Paris:
> https://open.spotify.com/artist/1Zw4aJCDjdFIgSEGKrteXj/discography
>
> Here is Milano Lounge - directly from Milan:
> https://www.milanoloungeradio.com/
>
> Here is Glenti FM - directly from Xanthi:
> https://www.glentifm.gr/

Destiny and Rationality

When Destiny and Rationality push together in the same direction, it could be impossible to resist.

This book was born out of an uncommon series of coincidences. I didn't talk about mostly of them, but I assure you that without those happenings, which occurred unexpectedly in certain precise moments of my life since several years ago, now I would not be here inside these pages; I'd be at the beach, instead. That series of moments produced this singularity. That is what Destiny did. A strong wind that blows towards a precise direction, so that it seems the only way to follow; that direction seems the only existent way. Nevertheless, if a person thinks rationally that it has to do other things, it can do other things - also against that strong wind.

But what happens if your Rationality also says that direction is what you have to do? If it says "that is right, do it"? If it says "now, or never"?

In that case, the strong wind becomes an hurricane. In this situation, it could become impossible to resist: you have to follow that way. You have to do what Destiny and Rationality, together, say.

This happened to me. In these days I had only to write and prepare this book. Anything else would have been an unnatural attempt to go against a hurricane.

Now, there is an important thing to say about: in cases like this, never forget the physical exercise. At least one hour of sport each day: jogging or, even better, bicycle (with uphills) are the simplest things that come to mind, but any other sport is good. If you can't do sport, take a one-hour outdoor walk. In addition there is the well-known rule, always good and fun-da-men-tal: do not sit for too long in a row. Get out of that chair often. Often. More often!

Do not stay inside your hurricane from the morning to the evening, otherwise serious damages could arrive - even hospital or worse - and if you will be damaged nothing can be done to finish your important work. Sitting all day long, or in any case doing the same thing all day long, is a serious danger to human life.

I wanted to show my experience about; because if it happens to you, you will be better prepared than - sadly - me and my family were.

Contacts

You can contact the Author of this book using the following web page:
futurbooks.com/hotel-train

to Giovanna, my mother

www.ingramcontent.com/pod-product-compliance
Lightning Source LLC
LaVergne TN
LVHW081541070526
838199LV00057B/3741